SS NIEUW AMSTERDAM

CLASSIC LINERS

SS NIEUW AMSTERDAM

ANDREW BRITTON

The History Press

First published 2015

The History Press
The Mill, Brimscombe Port
Stroud, Gloucestershire, GL5 2QG
www.thehistorypress.co.uk

British Library Cataloguing in Publication Data.
A catalogue record for this book is available from the British Library.

ISBN 978 0 7509 6102 8

Typesetting and origination by The History Press
Printed in China

I dedicate this book to Barry J. Eagles, who has given so much to promoting and encouraging interest in ocean liners and shipping, whilst actively preserving our maritime history.

Cover illustrations: Front: An aerial view of the SS *Nieuw Amsterdam* sailing from New York in August 1962; rear: Beauty beyond belief in the Bahamas as the SS *Nieuw Amsterdam* anchors off during the Christmas Caribbean Cruise of December 1950. (Both Holland America Line/Britton Collection)

Half title verso: The SS *Nieuw Amsterdam* is pictured at Hoboken dressed all over, ready for her South American voyage sailing from New York on 11 February 1939. (Britton Collection)

Contents

Introduction

From my earliest days the Holland America Line SS *Nieuw Amsterdam* was a familiar sight in Southampton Docks and around the Solent. I would frequently see this classic liner when travelling over to the Isle of Wight to visit my grandmother and indulge in my other great passion with steam trains. After leaving school I initially joined the police force and was lucky enough to go on a one-month international liaison attachment with the Netherlands Police. It was during this period that I was lucky enough to gain a closer acquaintance with the SS *Nieuw Amsterdam* at her home port in Rotterdam. The crew were very welcoming aboard and it was possible to explore the ship and afterwards enjoy a delicious meal. Although my family worked on the Cunard Line Atlantic liners, I developed a soft spot for the SS *Nieuw Amsterdam* and she became a favourite ship of mine. She was a beautifully elegant and well-proportioned ocean liner with a very high reputation for first-class comfort and standards aboard.

The original negative of this view of the SS *Nieuw Amsterdam* sailing from Le Havre was used for a postcard. (La Cigogne/Britton Collection)

My last sighting of the ship was back in Southampton – just a passing glimpse. She was always there, but then suddenly a memory. News filtered through the family grapevine via my Uncle Joe that the SS *Nieuw Amsterdam* had been sold for scrapping and the realisation dawned on me that I would never see her again. I therefore determined that I would like to find out more about her past and pay my own tribute to this magnificent Dutch classic liner. A chance discovery of her complete war records along with other British troopships opened the way to unlocking her hidden past.

On learning that I had embarked on researching the life story of the SS *Nieuw Amsterdam* I received tremendous encouragement and support from two friends: Barry J. Eagles, chairman of the SS *Shieldhall* Society and distinguished author, and Jim McFaul, the photographic archivist of the World Ship Society. These two gentlemen actively supported my endeavours and kept me going on the right course.

Acknowledgements

Tremendous encouragement and international support has been received in the writing of this book. This includes access to historical information and photographical material from the Holland America Line. The Canadian maritime historian Gordon Turner very generously mailed to me a large package of original historical documents and artefacts relating to the ship to assist with research and illustrations for the book. I can't thank Gordon enough. Additionally the Associated Press, British Ministry of Defence and the National Library of New Zealand have been extremely helpful in providing me with negatives and original prints of the SS *Nieuw Amsterdam* covering the career of the ship.

Special mention must be made of two other maritime stalwarts from the USA; David Boone and Ernest Arroyo have dipped into their archives to assist with photographic illustrations for this book.

Many friends have helped by allowing me include their original work and several have generously donated this material. I am indebted to Barry Eagles, Richard Weiss, Marche Piche, Ray Woodmore and Gavin Whitelaw as they have also given permission for their original work to be included and I am very grateful to them. Piet van Dijk has also been a source of great inspiration and encouragement with his enthusiasm and knowledge of the *SS Nieuw Amsterdam*. He has provided me with much historical information about the ship and directed me to many sources of information, for which I owe a great debt of thanks.

I must extend my sincere thanks to Richard Weiss, for providing me with a mass of black-and-white negatives, colour slides and original photographs of the ship to use in this book.

I owe a great debt of thanks to Jim McFaul of the World Ship Society for his considerable assistance in locating colour slides for this book.

I would like to extend my sincere thanks to the National Archives at Kew and Her Majesty's Ministry of Defence for providing me with considerable freedom to explore stored information and original records relating to the ship during her early service and in the Second World War. After delving through endless boxes of original records, my eyes almost popped out as I discovered the original records for the *SS Nieuw Amsterdam*, which had been hidden away and forgotten about since 1946. These unique records will become Crown copyright and be relocated to the National Archives at Kew; it is intended they will be open to public inspection at a future date when catalogued.

As always, my friend and neighbour Michael Jakeman has thoroughly checked the content of this book. I would like to express my appreciation for all his time, support and generous assistance.

I am extremely grateful to my brother-in-law Mike Pringle and my sister Ruth. A special thank you should go to my wife Annette, who spent many hours helping me. My sons Jonathan, Mark and Matthew are also owed a great debt of thanks for encouraging me and putting up with masses of colour slides and shipping artefacts.

In this smoky picture the SS *Nieuw Amsterdam* is seen passing her Holland America Line sister ship, SS *Statendam* at Rotterdam. (Britton Collection)

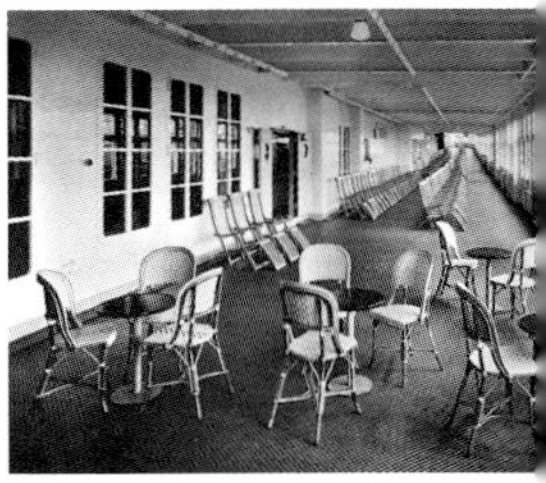

SS Nieuw Amsterdam Potted History

Design and Construction

The bleak world economic depression of the early 1930s damaged the fortunes of many shipping companies including the Holland America Line. By 1935 there was belief in an improving future and economic recovery. The Holland America Line, with sufficient financial funding from the Dutch government, proposed plans for a new, larger ship to partner and act as running mate for the 29,000-ton *SS Statendam* of 1929 on the transatlantic service from Rotterdam to New York. The proposed new liner was to be 'the ship of state' and pride of the nation, just as the 83,000-ton *Normandie* was to France, the 81,000-ton Cunard RMS *Queen Mary* was to Britain, the 51,000-ton *Rex* was to Italy and the 51,000-ton near-sisters *Bremen* and *Europa* were to Germany.

The Holland America Line did not plan to build the world's fastest or largest ocean liner to rival international competitors operating across the North Atlantic. Instead the Dutch designed and constructed a more moderate medium-sized vessel of 36,000 tons, which was not only capable of operating the transatlantic service, but also versatile enough to undertake profitable winter cruising to warmer climates. The construction of the new ship was to be undertaken in Holland, where employment could be offered to Dutch design teams, engineers and shipyard workers. The whole ethos of the construction of a new national flagship was looked upon as a morale boosting national prestige project during an era of emergence from a gloomy economic climate. Paramount to the thinking behind the new ship was that it was to become a floating symbol of all that was best in the Netherlands, in technology, national art and decoration.

Mr Ray Woodmore from the Isle of Wight has amongst his inimitable collection of ocean liner memorabilia this original and unique glass plate positive picture of the hull of SS *Nieuw Amsterdam* on the slipway at the launch ceremony in April 1937. (Ray Woodmore)

Under the command of Captain Johannes J. Bijl, the Master of the ship elect, the trials of the *Nieuw Amsterdam* commenced on the 23 April 1938 and were unusual as a large number of invited guests were on board for the four day trials. She is pictured here being hauled away from the quayside by local tugboats and watched by thousands along the shoreline. (Associated Press)

Previously the Holland America Line had earlier company liners constructed at the Harland & Wolff shipyard in Belfast, Northern Ireland. The political element of the provision of essential Dutch government loans to finance the new build ship was that it was essential that it would be built at home in Holland. Agreement was reached with the Rotterdam Dry Dock Company and contracts were signed and exchanged for the construction of the new ship for 13.5 million Guilders. The new ship was designated yard number 200. The keel was laid on 3 January 1936 and the Board of Holland America Line intended to name the new ship *Prisendam.* After much board room debate this name was changed. The selection of a more appropriate name of *Nieuw Amsterdam* was agreed. The new name was the name of the seventeenth-century Dutch settlement that became New York after British forces seized control in 1665.

The financing of the new-build ship was very constrained. In order to secure long-term employment the ship workers voluntarily agreed to a 2.5 per cent wage cut. It was therefore justifiably claimed that the new ship was paid for by the government of the Netherlands, Holland America Line and the Dutch people.

The keel was laid on 3 January 1936 with the building code 200. Towards the end of March 1937 the hull was almost ready for launching into the River Maas and preparations were made with dredging and the fitting of launch gear for the launch day on 10 April. The technicalities of the launch of the new ship were regarded as complex and demanding, so much so that a technical paper was written outlining the difficulties by G.M. Chambers, entitled, 'Launch of the Twin Screw Turbine Steamer *Nieuw Amsterdam*'. The launch weight of the hull of the ship was 18,200 tons. Ten bundles of drag chains were distributed on either side of the ship totalling 886 tons. The maximum speed of the ship during the launch sequence was 27ft per second.

Thousands of patriotic Dutch spectators witnessed Her Majesty Queen Wilhelmina of the Netherlands christen and launch the new ship, *Nieuw Amsterdam.* At the launching reception Queen Wilhelmina raised her glass and offered the following toast: 'To the common good and the safe journey of the new ship, the *Nieuw Amsterdam*, I propose this toast.' The Dutch Minister of Economic Affairs, Henri Gelissen, said in reply: 'God grant that this first happy launching of the flagship of the Dutch merchant navy may be a good omen, signalling a prosperous journey into the future. May the *Nieuw Amsterdam* carry the Dutch Tricolour wide and long across the seas for the glory and benefit of our beloved country.'

Interior Design

My grandfather was invited aboard the Nieuw Amsterdam whilst she was docked in Hoboken and praised the interior design, in particular. Dutch artists had queued to contribute to the distinctive décor of the new ship amongst whom were:

Cor Alons: stained glass in third-class bar and tourist-class children's playroom
Eva Besnyö: photo wall in third-class smoking room
Pieter den Besten: decorative panel in purser's office
Herman Bieling: oil painting in chief engineer's lounge
Elisabeth de Boer: six luxury cabins and the theatre on the promenade deck
Leen Bolle: metal and plastic in the tourist-class lounge
Leo Brom: copper-plated panel in the cabin-class main deck reception hall
Jan Eloy Brom: copper-plated panel in the cabin-class main deck reception hall
Hildegard Brom-Fischer: hand-knotted rug for under the panel referred to above
Dirk Bus: sculpture in the tourist-class dining room
Heinrich Campendonk: glass painting at rear of third-class lounge
Agnes Canta: murals at rear of cabin-class theatre
Joseph Cantré: carved pilasters in the cabin-class dining room
Henk Chabot: painting of master in reception
Paul Citroen: glass paintings in cocktail bar and cabin-class verandas
Joan Collette: two paintings in cabin-class card room and writing room/library
Andries Copier: etched glass panel in tourist-class dining room (with others)
Cornelis Engelen: architect of theatre and a number of cabins (with Elizabeth de Boer), lounges of chief engineer and chief officer, and other interior components
Frits Eschauzier: designer of the cabin-class smoking room and its cocktail bar
Charles Eyck: twenty etched glass panes in the grand hall (with Henk Wouda)
Corinne Franzen-Heslenfeld: bronze figurine in luxury cabin 59
Jaap Gidding: lacquer painting and carpets (in collaboration with others, including Andries Copier)
Willem Gispen: seats
Mevrouw R. Gispen-van de Griend: mirrored bathroom floors
Frits van Hall: wooden sculpture in the rear of the promenade deck lounge
Jan Hendriks: tourist-class café bar and the adjoining veranda, and foyers of cabin-class main deck, promenade deck, and A and B decks
Siem van den Hoonaard: beaten bronze artifact in tourist-class lobby
Han Hulsbergen: two large paintings for the Ritz Carlton
Harry Kammer: luxury cabin 60 (designed together with his wife)
Mrs. J. Kammer-Kret: luxury cabin 60 (designed together with her husband)

Top left: An interior view of the first-class cinema in March 1953. (Britton Collection)

Above: An interior view of the first-class staircase, in March 1953. (Britton Collection)

Top right: An interior view of the first-class grand hall in March 1953. (Britton Collection)

Charles Karsten: interior stateroom 62 (with Ben Merkelbach)
Nel Klaassen: various decorations
Adriaan Lubbers: two large paintings in cabin-class dining room
Ben Merkelbach: interior stateroom 62 (with Charles Karsten)
William Molin: six aluminum 'plaques' on patina panels in tourist-class promenade lounge
Chris de Moor: Semipalatinsk Gobelin in cabin-class dining room
Joep Nicolas: various *vermurails* (glass wall paintings), opaline- and stained-glass decorations
Wim Nijs: two ornamental railings on the Ritz Carlton veranda in cabin class and an ivory chapel crucifix
Toon Ninaber van Eyben: painting in Chief Steward's reception room
Erna van Osselen: watercolour for the cabin-class dining room front lobby
James Old: tourist-class lounge and cigar lounge and cabin-class pool interiors
Henri Polak: carpet of tourist-class lounge
Johan Polet: ceiling supports, in bronze and aluminum, of the pilasters in the Grand Hall
John Raedecker: embossed ceiling panels and ornamental panels in the Grand Hall, and wall sculptures in tourist-class smoking room
Sybold of Ravesteyn: third-class dining room and tourist-class library/reading room decor
Han Adjusters: wood sculpture in third-class library/reading room
Marius Richters: oil painting in senior officer's reception room
Lode Sengers: four painted panels on tourist-class bar veranda

Above: An interior view of the first-class promenade deck in March 1953. (Britton Collection)

Top Left: An interior view of the first-class smoking room in March 1953. (Britton Collection)

Top Right: An interior view of the first-class solarium in March 1953. (Britton Collection)

Lambert Simon: various bas-reliefs in third-class dining room
Elisabeth Spanier-Dammers: among others, a plated copper frieze in cabin-class pool
Frits Spaniard: design of a number of rooms, many in third class
Pieter Starreveld: carved pillar in the Ritz Carlton cocktail lounge:
Reijer Stolk: a lacquer panel at cabin-class theatre entrance
Albert Termote: bronze bas-relief of Queen Wilhelmina in the cabin-class lobby
Han Wezelaar: silvered bronze sculptures in the tourist-class smoking room
Piet van der Wilt: decorative painting on staircase leading to the Ritz Carlton
Piet Worm: decor in tourist-class games room
Henk Wouda: furnishings in two luxury cabins
Ellen Wijdeveld Chasubles for Sunday mass in the chapel
Hendrik Wijdeveld: various rooms
Ruscha Wijdeveld: decor of cabin-class games room, including stained-glass windows.

As recognition and appreciation for these many assignments the Holland America Line commissioned the Dutch Art Association to produce a commemorative bronze statue, the *Nude with Flower* by Henk Chabot. The statue was placed on the stairs in the departure hall and the unveiling took place on 8 March 1940. During the Second World War the statue disappeared. In 1998, a copy of the statue on the stairs was presented to the cruise terminal located at the Wilhelminakade in Rotterdam.

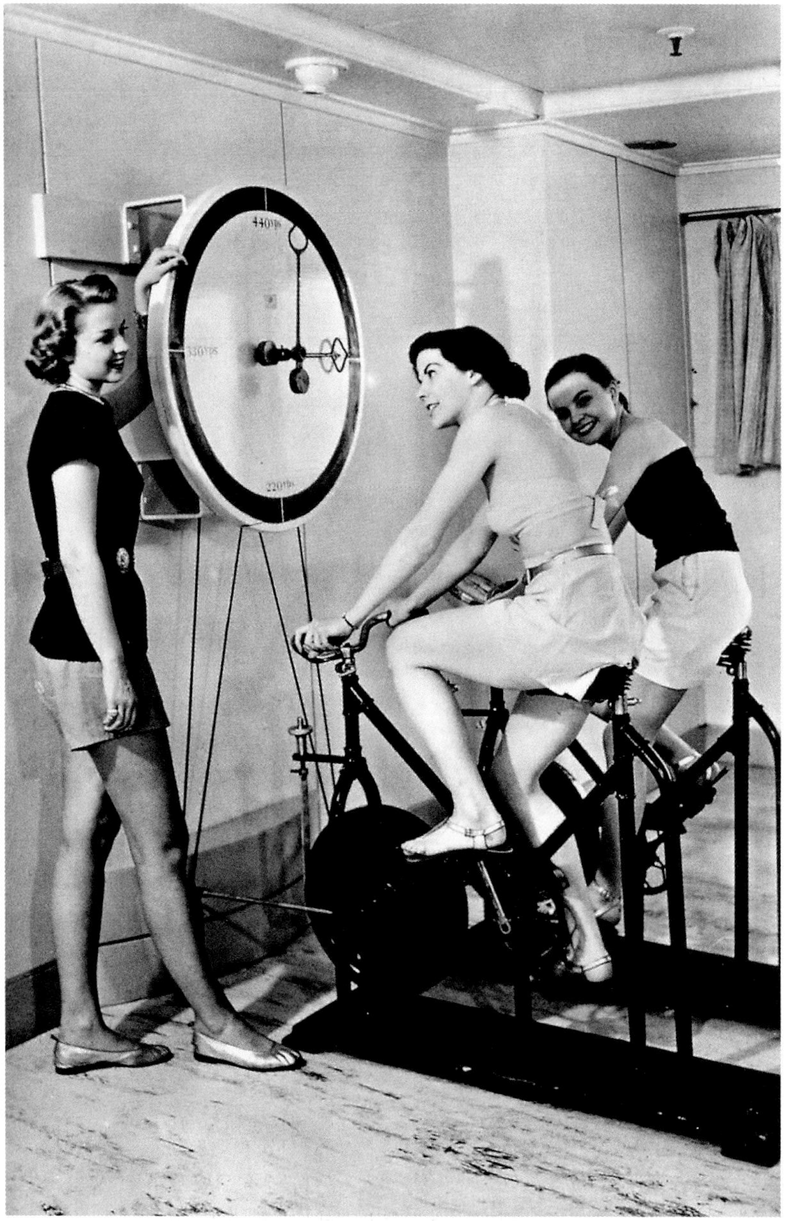

The ship was decorated in the Art Deco trend. The ethos of the new liner was further characterised by light, elegance and a truly modern look. It also received the nickname, *'ship of tomorrow'*. A highlight in the interior of the ship was the first restaurant, with a ceiling lined with Moroccan leather and Murano glass, and pillars covered with gold leaf. One of the two pools on board was Delft blue tile. The ship also had a theatre with air conditioning and a design based on the latest acoustic insights. At the entrance to the theatre for cabin class was a decorative lakpaneel in red, black, gold and maroon of Reijerzoon Stolk. At the time of construction, there was only one other passenger ship with its own theatre, the French *Normandie*. Also unique at that time was the fact that first-class passengers could have a private en suite bathroom.

Following the initial fitting out of the ship it was towed by ten tugs to the floating dry dock at the nearby Wilton Fijenoord Shipyard. Once safely in the floating dry dock, the ship's single 33-ton balanced rudder and two three-bladed 23-ton manganese bronze propellers were installed. Meanwhile all drag chains and launching gear was carefully removed. Next the hull of the ship was painted with red oxide paint, followed by several coats of matt grey-coloured undercoat and gloss black topcoats, prior to return to the builders for final completion. In mid-March all boilers were steamed and certified, followed by a quayside technical testing from 21 to 24 March.

Above: An interior view of the first-class gymnasium in March 1953. (Britton Collection)

Right: An interior view of a first-class double cabin in March 1953. (Britton Collection)

Trials and Maiden Voyage

Under the command of Captain Johannes J. Bijl, the master of the ship elect, the trials of the *Nieuw Amsterdam* commenced on 23 April 1938. Unusually, a large number of invited guests were on board for the four-day trials. Amongst the distinguished names on the guest list were Dr Hendrik Colijin, the Prime Minister of the Netherlands, and members of the Dutch Cabinet, the British ambassador Sir Charles Hubert Montgomery, the ambassadors of Belgium, France and Germany and the board members of the Holland America Line. The sea trials were undertaken in the English Channel and North Sea, and the ship returned to Rotterdam to prepare for her maiden voyage. Amateur black-and-white cine film taken off the south coast of England of the trials shows the *Nieuw Amsterdam* increasing speed to 22.8 knots at 131rpm on 35,100shp.

On returning to port, all instruments, machinery and boilers were thoroughly inspected and although some parts were identified as being 'stiff', the ship was signed off as 'fit for purpose'. Over the next three weeks the *Nieuw Amsterdam* was now prepared for her maiden voyage. She sailed from Rotterdam on the 10 May 1938 watched by thousands from every vantage point. Proud Dutch well-wishers cheered and waved while tugs and vessels enthusiastically saluted with their ship's whistles and sirens as the new pride of the Dutch nation sailed majestically past, heading outbound to Boulogne, Southampton and west across the North Atlantic to New York.

The rapturous welcome in New York for the maiden voyage arrival of the *Nieuw Amsterdam* was ecstatic and euphoric. Fireboats shot plumes of spray up into the sky above the ship as a traditional New York salute to a

This Holland America half-plate negative was used to produce official postcards showing the trial voyage from Rotterdam on 23 April 1938. (Britton Collection)

When the appeal went out for help with illustrations for this book, the *New York Times* generously responded by sending this photograph from their archives showing the maiden voyage entry into New York on the 16 May 1938. The *New York Times* reporter from 1938 had captioned the picture with a note that the liner had taken 5 days, 23 hours and 45 minutes to cross the Atlantic. (Associated Press)

new liner. After passing through the Narrows, the new Dutch liner slowly steamed up the Hudson to a deafening crescendo of whistles from local tugs, ferries and other liners docked at the piers. The ship had taken 5 days, 23 hours and 45 minutes at an average speed of 21.7 knots. At some stages of the maiden voyage the *Nieuw Amsterdam* reached 23 knots.

The naval architect, Sir William Isherwood, who was sailing aboard as an observer, commented: 'She's as safe and strong as a ship can be. We had a bit of pitching sea the second day out, and last night a rolling sea. But she rode well and is a very, very steady ship.' The New York newspapers reported: 'In marked contrast to her conventional black hull and white superstructure the accommodation were so extremely modernistic that many persons heralded it as a new school of decorating.' Over the next few days the *Nieuw Amsterdam* was tied up and 'open house' for inspection between 10 a.m. and 1 p.m. for $1 per person, with all proceeds being donated to local seamen's charities. Curious New Yorkers flocked to tour the ship and there were many favourable comments from the visitors.

The *Nieuw Amsterdam* had now joined the Holland America Line's *Statendam* and the old *Rotterdam* on the main North Atlantic service. The Dutch shipping line's *Noordam* and *Zaadam* joined the fleet as tourist ships and the *Volendam* and *Veendam* worked the intermediate service. With the *Pennland* and *Westernland* operating from Antwerp, the Holland America Line looked in fine shape for future growth and demand.

Responding to an SOS distress call on 30 June 1938, the *Nieuw Amsterdam* – which was on a westbound voyage to New York – swung south-west off its course. It sailed at full speed to rendezvous with the SS *Canford Chine*, which was heading out of Norfolk, VA, eastbound across the Atlantic to Swansea Docks in South Wales. Unfortunately, this small tramp steamer carried no ship's physician. When on the scene, the *Nieuw Amsterdam* stopped all engines and lowered a lifeboat manned by volunteers from the ship's crew. They rowed across to the SS *Canford Chine* to rescue Feliks Kuuseoks, an Estonian sailor who was severely injured after falling from scaffolding. He was safely transferred to the *Nieuw Amsterdam*'s lifeboat and returned to the *Nieuw Amsterdam* to receive urgent medical attention.

Later in 1938, on her sixth voyage, the *Nieuw Amsterdam* set a new record for the run between New York and Rotterdam of 6 days, 13 hours and 18 minutes. In October 1938 the new Dutch flagship arrived in New York to discover that she had to dock without the assistance of tugs owing to a strike. This demanded great skill and confidence, knowledge of the local tides and winds and a vast experience of seamanship. The captain

Left: A striking portrait picture of Commodore Johann Jacobs Bijl, master of the SS *Nieuw Amsterdam*, taken aboard his ship at New York. (Associated Press)

Above: A spectacular aerial view of the maiden voyage arrival in New York of the SS *Nieuw Amsterdam* on 16 May 1938. (Britton Collection)

of the *Nieuw Amsterdam* had to patiently wait for the exact moment of still water between the tides, whilst waiting on the Hudson. Very carefully and gingerly he then manoeuvred the enormous 36,287-ton liner's bow into the neck of the pier and used it to pivot the vessel into position. Once securing lines had been thrown to waiting hands on the pier, the ship was slowly hauled in and made secure. At any point during this delicate manoeuvre a sudden gust of wind, change in the current or tide could have brought untold disaster on the ship and pier. Watching from the shore were members of the tugboat crews waiting for any sudden wrong move. As the *Nieuw Amsterdam* berthed without incident the watching crowds burst in to cheering applause. The captain responded with a burst of three whistles, probably in great relief at his successful manoeuvre. This was the first occasion that the *Nieuw Amsterdam* was required to dock in New York without the assistance of tugs, but it would not be the last in her long career. As soon as the North Atlantic summer season of 1938 was finished, the *Nieuw Amsterdam* started to make cruises from New York to South America and the Caribbean, passing through the Panama Canal.

Above: Mid-Atlantic drama with the rescue of Feliks Kuuseoks, an Estonian sailor from the SS *Canford Chine*, pictured being transferred aboard the SS *Nieuw Amsterdam* on 30 June 1938. (Associated Press)

Right: During the first few pre-war voyages the SS *Nieuw Amsterdam* carried many famous celebrities across the Atlantic. For the eastward maiden voyage from New York on 21 May 1938, the ship carried the celebrated Dutch violinist Leni Van Thijn and her 4-year-old daughter, Ruth. Leni Van Thijn founded the first female string quartet in the Netherlands and she is pictured here at the start of her four-month European tour. (Associated Press)

Second World War

1939

From around the time of the dock trials of the *Nieuw Amsterdam* in March 1938 a dark cloud of uncertainty had began to descend across Europe when on 13 March 1938 Nazi Germany annexed Austria. Fears were temporarily alleviated on 30 September 1938 with the signing of the Munich Agreement, which allowed Germany to annex the Sudetenland of Czechoslovakia. However, when German troops occupied the remainder of Czechoslovakia on 15 March 1939 many evacuees began to escape Europe to the USA on the *Nieuw Amsterdam.* When the German Führer Adolf Hitler demanded the port of Danzig, leading to the invasion of Poland and outbreak of war on 1 September 1939, the trickle of passengers heading across the Atlantic on the *Nieuw Amsterdam* became a roaring torrent of people escaping the conflict in Europe.

It was decided by the board of Holland America Line and the Dutch government that after only seventeen and a half transatlantic voyages it would be safer for the *Nieuw Amsterdam* to temporarily cease operations across the 'big pond'. She was laid up at Hoboken Pier in New York Harbour.

On 4 September 1939 at Hoboken, large 6ft-high white letters, '*Nieuw Amsterdam,* Holland' were painted along her sides to indicate that this was a vessel sailing from a neutral country. The following day she sailed to Rotterdam. At the end of her return voyage to New York, the ship

The postcard caption says it all: 'Transiting the Panama Canal'. (Britton Collection)

Top left: This spectacular night-time shot of the SS *Nieuw Amsterdam* taken on Tuesday, 14 March, 1939 shows her illuminated at Rio de Janeiro berthed next to the Touring Club at the foot of the Avenida Rio Branco, one of the principal streets. (Dr. H.C. Fulton/ Britton Collection)

Above: The SS *Nieuw Amsterdam* is seen resting at berth on Wednesday, 15 March, 1939 at the foot of the Avenida Rio Branco and the Brazilian Touring Club, Rio de Janeiro. Note the splendid line-up of pre-war vehicles. (Dr. H.C. Fulton/Britton Collection)

Left: Monday 27 March 1939 finds the *Nieuw Amsterdam* in idyllic setting of Caracas Harbour at Curaçao. (Dr H.C. Fulton/Britton Collection)

Right: The view from the shore on Monday 27 March 1939. (Dr H.C. Fulton/ Britton Collection)

Far right: After sailing from Rio the ship was at sea on Friday 17 March 1939 where the passengers enjoyed a fancy dress evening. They are pictured here on deck. (Dr H.C. Fulton/ Britton Collection)

Above: Crossing the equator on the SS *Nieuw Amsterdam* in 1939. This picture shows King Neptune's Court, near the swimming pool, where one of the subjects is due to receive an early bath! (Dr H.C. Fulton/Britton Collection)

Below: As there were not facilities for the SS *Nieuw Amsterdam* at St Thomas, in the Virgin Islands, she anchored off. Passengers wishing to go ashore on Saturday, 25 March, 1939 were conveyed to the landing quay at Charlotte Amalie via the liner's lifeboats. (Dr H.C. Fulton/Britton Collection)

was temporarily laid up and 'mothballed' at Hoboken. After a few weeks of inactivity, the ship was reactivated to cruise in safer waters from New York to Bermuda, the Bahamas and the Caribbean. Instead of leaving the ship laid up, a number of cruises were made in the American hemisphere. Between 21 October and 18 November, cruises were made to Bermuda, followed by another series, starting with the Christmas Cruise from 23 December, to the Caribbean. As these initial cruises were successful, the neutral ship kept cruising for the whole of the winter of 1939–40, but with the uncertainties of early 1940, bookings rapidly dipped.

Left: This was the scene at the quayside at Hoboken on 5 September 1939 as the *Nieuw Amsterdam* sailed to Rotterdam. She was carrying just 225 passengers to the Netherlands and sailed with 6ft-high white letters painted on both sides of her hull. The stops on this voyage at Plymouth and Boulogne were cancelled and she sailed direct to Rotterdam. (Associated Press)

Above: With the war threatening in Europe, many famous politicians, writers and artists decided to flee to the United States. Amongst them, travelling on the SS *Nieuw Amsterdam* on 29 September 1939, was John Gunther, the author of *Inside of Europe* and *Inside of Asia*. (Associated Press)

Left: The painters are pictured at work at Hoboken on 5 September 1939, painting 6ft high letters on the side of the SS *Nieuw Amsterdam*, prior to sailing. This was a precaution for sailing into the so-called 'warzone' to indicate Dutch neutrality. (Associated Press)

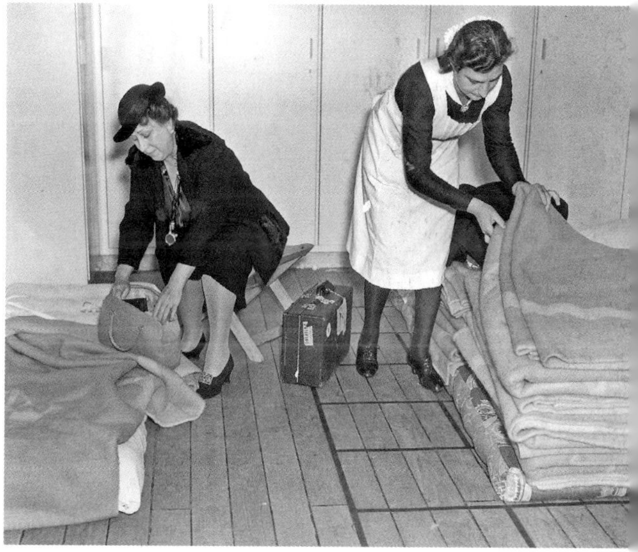

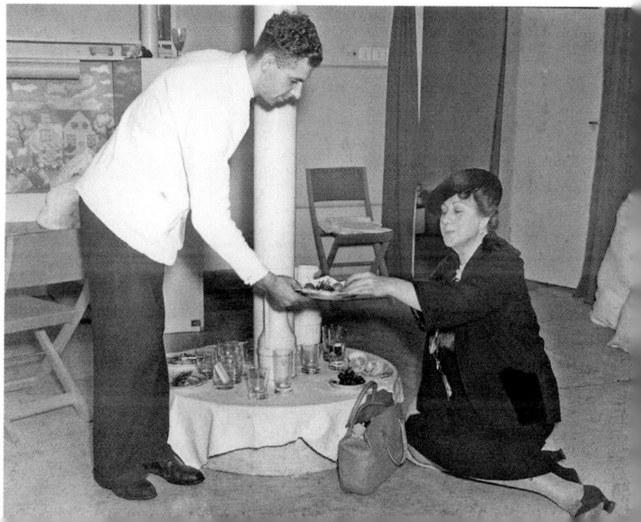

Above: A group of 116 smiling Hollanders are pictured on the decks of the SS *Nieuw Amsterdam* shortly after arriving at New York on 21 July 1939. The group from Flushing had arrived for the World's Fair and to tour Canada. With the onset of war in Europe, many of the group decided to remain in the USA. Theodore E. Tresfon, chief steward of the SS *Nieuw Amsterdam* is pictured on the front row of the group on the left. (Associated Press)

Top right: As the clouds of war gathered in Europe, many Jews and politicians decided to escape to the USA. The voyage in early September was packed with every space occupied. Here stewardess Leah Westbrink of the SS *Nieuw Amsterdam* replaces mattresses and cushions from the children's playroom, which had been converted into an emergency dormitory on 6 September 1939. (Associated Press)

Centre: With the outbreak of the Second World War now imminent the westbound voyage of the SS *Nieuw Amsterdam* was packed. Sailing into New York on 1 September 1939 she carried 1,286 refugees. Special dormitories for women and men were set up in various parts of the ship to accommodate the exodus. Here SS *Nieuw Amsterdam* Stewardess Leah Westbrink assists Jewish refugee passenger Mrs Jacques Jacobs, who has camped out on the floor. (Associated Press)

Right: With 1,286 lucky refugee passengers on board, the SS *Nieuw Amsterdam* set sail to New York, arriving on 1 September 1939. Every space was occupied and in this view Mrs Jacques Jacobs, a Jewish refugee, is seen being served by a steward as she sits on the floor of the children's playroom. (Associated Press)

Left: The 1,286 passengers escaping the conflict in Europe in early September 1939 and sailing on the SS *Nieuw Amsterdam* brought with them their treasured possessions – as much as they could carry. This rare view taken at New York on 1 September shows the mass of baggage crammed on the Main Deck. (Associated Press)

Relief, despair, fear and uncertainty. A truly historic and very rare photograph that conveys the feelings at this desperate time, more than any words that could be written. This was the unique scene at the arrival pier in New York, where refugee passengers escaping the outbreak of the Second World War piled off the SS *Nieuw Amsterdam*. The relatives and friends of the passengers added to the throng. (Associated Press)

1940

During the so-called 'phoney war' between September 1939 and May 1940, Holland was officially neutral and at peace. In theory the *Nieuw Amsterdam* was under no threat of attack from German U-boats or surface raiders. On 10 May 1940 six of Holland America Line's vessels were lying at berth in the port of Rotterdam. They were: the liners *Statendam* and *Veendam*, and the cargo ships *Damsterdyk Dinteldyk* and *Boshdyk*. Despite its policy of neutrality, the Netherlands was invaded by the Germans on the morning of 10 May 1940 without a formal declaration of war. The Dutch military, with insufficient weapons and equipment, was caught unprepared. The German forces advanced rapidly across Holland. Four days later, the German commander presented an ultimatum to the Dutch commander of Rotterdam commanding the city to surrender but as it was being presented the city was bombed by the Luftwaffe, killing 800–900 civilians. The Holland America Line attempted to move its vessels to safety, but German seaplanes had already landed on the River Maas, capturing bridges and blocking the harbour with magnetic mines. In the crossfire the three-funnelled *Statendam* caught fire and was gutted over the next five days. Her wreck was later towed away by the Germans for scrapping and recycling of metal for German armaments.

News of the invasion and bombing of Rotterdam reached the *Nieuw Amsterdam* on the other side of the Atlantic. While the ship was sailing from La Guaira to Puerto Cabellon on 10 May 1940, a signal arrived with the unbelievable news that the Netherlands had been invaded and it was possible that the country may fall. A second signal confirmed that the Dutch government had fled the country into exile and had secretly escaped across the Channel to London. Furthermore, Her Majesty Queen Wilhelmina had escaped in the night carrying the crown jewels of the Netherlands.

An immediate reaction to these dramatic developments in Europe came from the Holland America Line New York Office in Lower Broadway, which signalled to the Nieuw Amsterdam: 'Return to port in all haste STOP Cruise cancelled STOP Await further instructions on arrival at 5th Street Hoboken STOP M Jol'.

According to former Staff Captain Rens Brandson, the mood dramatically changed on board the *Nieuw Amsterdam.* There was shock that the ship was now at war and it was felt that she could be under threat of attack from German U-boats. Captain Bijl ordered a change of course heading towards New York and increased to full speed, following a zigzag pattern.

Captain Brandson recalled with some emotion:

> All I could think about was my wife, Margaretha, and our two daughters back home in Rotterdam now living under the control of the German jackboot. From this point on I did not hear from them for five years. I did not know if they were alive or not, and they had no knowledge of me.

On learning of the bombing of the port of Rotterdam, the mood on board the *Nieuw Amsterdam* changed again to one of anger!

On arrival at the Holland America Line at Hoboken, the *Nieuw Amsterdam's* passengers were quickly transferred ashore and issued with a letter from the company expressing regret for the cancellation of the cruise and offering full compensation. Those on board recall departing passengers warmly wishing the crew and ship well with handshakes and even hugs. The empty ship was now laid up and under the guard of local mounted police and a patrol car.

With the Dutch now involved in the conflict it was to be expected that the *Nieuw Amsterdam* would be called up for war duty. This process took a while, as the Dutch government which had fled the country at the last possible moment had to re-establish itself. For a short time the Dutch affairs were temporarily run from Curaçao in the Dutch West Indies, but a permanent seat 'in exile' was eventually set up in London, where Queen Wilhelmina had also settled. A number of exiled European governments were now based in London and together with the USA they would later on form the Allied Forces. It took some time to get it all properly established and organised, but by September the government-in-exile's thoughts had focused on the Dutch merchant marine and how its ships could contribute and play a part in the war effort. Thus on 12 September 1940, the *Nieuw Amsterdam* was officially seized by the Dutch government-in-exile and transferred to British Ministry of War Transport. During the First World War the Kingdom of the Netherlands had remained neutral, which meant that when in 1917 the USA seized the Dutch ships in a similar way the Dutch crews had to leave their ships and were returned to Holland. Now, with Holland involved in the war, the Dutch crew of the *Nieuw Amsterdam* could stay and participate fully in the future liberation effort. For administration purposes, the *Nieuw Amsterdam* was placed under Cunard White Star management, but it remained under the Dutch flag and continued to sail with a Dutch crew. From this point the ship was officially registered as HMT *Nieuw Amsterdam* until the 1946. (Source: HM Ministry of Defence, London)

Between May and September, whilst in New York, the ship was moved from berth to berth a few times. During one of these manoeuvres the ship collided with two other vessels due to the strong winds blowing down the Hudson River. Although the damage was considered unsubstantial, the repair bill still ran to $100,000. The *Nieuw Amsterdam* entered Todd's Shipyard graving dock in the Erie Basin, Brooklyn, for repair and a coat of matt-grey paint all over. At 758ft in length, the *Nieuw Amsterdam* was the largest vessel to use the graving dock and it was a very tight squeeze to fit in. Consequently the outer dock gates had to remain open to allow for the overhang of the bow and stern. During the time the ship was undergoing repair regular security patrols with guard dogs were undertaken and security was intense to deter any possible attack by local German undercover agents.

Unannounced and under cover of darkness on the evening of 12 September, the *Nieuw Amsterdam* slipped her moorings at New York and silently sailed down the Hudson and out through the Narrows. On board were a new crew under the command of Holland America Line Captain John J. Ax. The black, two-funnel silhouette was observed sailing north; her destination Halifax, Canada.

Arriving at Halifax the following day on 13 September, the first task was to fit degaussing equipment around the hull in order to repel magnetic mines. Additionally, thirty-six guns were fitted, including a former 6in British gun, four 4in anti-aircraft guns, machine guns and Oerlikons. Whilst being manoeuvred from her arrival berth in Halifax, the British Ministry of Defence records state that the ship was involved in a collision on 31 September. She sailed from Halifax bound for Singapore on 11 October, calling at Cape Town in Table Bay, South Africa on 26 October for refuelling and replenishment of fresh water. Here, army personnel boarded the *Nieuw Amsterdam* to become her armed resident support crew.

During the Second World War there were seven troopships that were capable of sailing fast without escorts and they were officially codenamed 'monsters'. These were the former British Cunard *Queen Mary*, *Queen Elizabeth*, *Mauretania*, *Aquitania*, former French *Ile de France* and *Pasteur* and the former Dutch *Nieuw Amsterdam*. Their every movement throughout the course of the Second World War was to be closely monitored in the War Office at Whitehall, with regular reports made to the British Prime Minister Winston Churchill about their secret movements.

The *Nieuw Amsterdam* entered Singapore on 9 November where the removal of many of the luxury fixtures and fittings ashore commenced to place them into store for the duration of the war. Meanwhile carpenters, plumbers and fitters set to work on converting the ship's peacetime cabins and staterooms into military dormitories to accommodate up to 6,000 troops. From 7 December, tiers of steel bunks were erected and secured to the deck floors and walls. Where possible the tiers of bunks were separated by a mere 3ft, in order to increase capacity. Communal latrines and washroom facilities were hastily converted from all available spaces on the ship. The cinema and the beautiful grand hall followed a similar fate and were transformed into large dormitories. An inspection for readiness for sea was carried out on board on 21 December and refuelling, loading of supplies of food and fresh water was undertaken on the 22–23 December in readiness to set sail the following day on Christmas Eve bound for Sydney, Australia. The logbook records that the ship passed Thursday Island on 29 December and arrived safely in Sydney on 2 January 1941.

1941

Whilst at Sydney, from 2 January 1941, the crew were given limited shore leave. Upon returning to the ship, permission was granted to the crew and army personnel to jump from the promenade deck in to the sea and swim around the ship to re-enter via a Jacob's ladder at the shell door. On two occasions an alarm bell was sounded recalling those swimming to immediately rejoin the ship as sharks had been observed nearby!

From midnight of 21 January the ship was transferred to the command of STA1 for the conveyance of New Zealand and Australian troops to the Middle East theatre of war. Throughout the day of 22 January the *Nieuw Amsterdam* was refuelled and restocked with food and water supplies in readiness to sail the following day to Auckland and Wellington. She arrived in Wellington on 27 January where several thousand brave Kiwi members of the 2 New Zealand Expeditionary Force in their traditional 'lemon squeezer' hats and high-collared khaki uniforms were waiting quayside to board. Within an hour of tying up, boarding commenced and the loading of military equipment went on relentlessly until the ship sailed on 1 February, returning to Sydney at speed two days later.

Upon arriving in Sydney, the New Zealand troops remained on board the *Nieuw Amsterdam*. In Sydney Harbour, the Dutch troopship rendezvoused with the RMS *Queen Mary* (HMT *QX*), which had embarked 6,000 Australian troops the night before and the RMS *Aquitania*. The three liners were classified as 'monsters' and they met at Sydney Heads. Escorted by HMAS *Hobart* they sailed for Melbourne as Convoy US9. They were joined by RMS *Mauretania* in the Bass Strait on 6 February and sailed bound for Fremantle, arriving on the 9 February. The convoy continued their voyage on 2 February, joined by another escort, HMAS Canberra. The troops on board the RMS Queen Mary were heading for the Middle East. A few days out from Fremantle the RMS Queen Mary, which was at the head of Convoy US9, swung around from behind the other ships. She then came alongside close and those on board cheered and saluted before the Queen Mary for a farewell pass. The three other liners turned and headed for Bombay, where the troops aboard were transferred to other smaller vessels.

Following a swift turn around at Bombay, the *Nieuw Amsterdam* sailed for a return to Fremantle on 26 February, calling at Colombo on the 1 March. The locally prepared curry meals from Bombay consumed on board on the evening of the 26 February were to have devastating consequences as it is reported there were reports of dysentery and sickness throughout the ship. On arrival at Fremantle on 15 March, the ship was thoroughly disinfected. The *Nieuw Amsterdam* set sail again within 48 hours on 17 March bound for Sydney, where she docked on 21 March. Her stay was short-lived, for the next day she sailed with the RMS *Mauretania* across the Tasman Sea to Wellington in New Zealand, arriving there on 30 March.

Berthing in King's Wharf, *Mauretania* on the western side, *Nieuw Amsterdam* on the eastern side, 4,400 New Zealand troops boarded the *Mauretania* and 2,590 troops embarked on the *Nieuw Amsterdam*. The *Nieuw Amsterdam* logbook records that the two ships sailed from Wellington on the 7 April and were escorted by the cruisers HMAS *Achilles*, HMAS *Australia* and HMAS *Hobart*. Meanwhile back in Sydney, Australian troops were assembled for embarkation on the three other 'monster' ships: RMS *Queen Mary* with 6,000 troops, RMS *Queen Elizabeth* with 5,333 troops and the SS *Ile de France* with 3,271 troops. This was the first time that both Cunard Queen liners operated together. The *Nieuw Amsterdam* and the *Mauretania* arrived at Sydney on 10 April. The *Nieuw Amsterdam* took on board a further 1,213 Australian troops, raising her total complement to 3,803 men.

At 7 a.m. on 11 April, the *Queen Elizabeth* raised anchor and set sail on her maiden trooping voyage Convoy US10. She was followed by: *Ile de France, Mauretania* and *Nieuw Amsterdam,* at a distance of 1,000 yards apart. Although this was supposed to be a closely guarded secret, hundreds of small craft escorted the four 'monsters' out of Sydney Harbour, some waving banners with the words, 'God Bless the Sixth Div. Cav.' and 'Good luck 2/3 MG Bn'. Once out into open water off Jervis Bay, the four troopships rendezvoused with the *Queen Mary*. Closely watched by circling aerial escorts overhead, Convoy US10 then assembled into formation: *Queen Mary* on the starboard side, *Queen Elizabeth* in the middle and *Mauretania* on her port side, with the *Ile de France* following behind *Queen Mary* and *Nieuw Amsterdam* behind the *Mauretania*. The columns were kept 1,000 yards apart with the two following troopships maintaining a gap of 800 yards from the leading ships. This was the largest troop-carrying convoy of the Second World War. Convoy US10 maintained 19 knots and headed towards Fremantle arriving there on 16 April. The two gigantic Cunard Queens anchored off in Gages Roads, while the other three troopships entered port and berthed. Although the three ships remained in port for three days no shore leave was given to those on board. The conditions on board the cramped *Ile de France* were worsened by the addition of a further 778 troops.

The total number being carried on the troopships of Convoy US10 was now 22,000 men. They were escorted from Fremantle by the Australian cruisers *Australia, Canberra* and *Sydney*. Once clear of the coast, the three columns of troopships increased their speed across the Indian Ocean to 20 knots.

All had not been well on the *Ile de France* since the voyage commenced. There was a major problem with the food, which was prepared by Asian cooks in the kitchens. The meals consisted mostly of boiled potatoes. The Asian cooks were used to preparing rice-based meals laced with large quantities of chillies. This menu had been only slightly adapted, with the rice being substituted by potatoes. The result of this diet after a week at sea was a near mutiny by the New Zealand and Australian troops aboard. After an exchange of words in a meeting with the officers on board, the cooks were replaced with Australian and New Zealand Army staff.

The situation on board the *Nieuw Amsterdam* was little better with cramped conditions, poor-quality food and restricted physical activity. There were reports of fighting and arguments amongst troops aboard the Dutch ship. The humid heat and smell from latrines added to the frustration aboard.

Three days out from Fremantle on 22 April, the *Nieuw Amsterdam* exchanged visual signals with the ships in the convoy, as there was strict radio silence for communication between the ships. The Dutch troopship then changed course and headed at an increased speed to Singapore. On arrival at Singapore, the Australian troops aboard all disembarked to reinforce the local garrison. The New Zealand troops meanwhile transferred to the Cunard *Aquitania*, which had just emerged from the dry dock. The four-funnel *Aquitania* raised steam and sailed for Colombo to join up with Convoy US10. The *Nieuw Amsterdam* remained at Singapore until 9 May. The logbook states that during this time the vessel underwent extensive repairs.

The *Nieuw Amsterdam* sailed from Singapore on 9 May bound for Bombay arriving on the 15th and sailing on 18 May, Mombassa in Kenya arriving on the 23rd and sailing on 24 May and before docking in Durban, South Africa on 28 May. Further repairs to the ship were undertaken in Durban and she sailed again on 10 June with South African troops bound for Suez where she arrived on 20 June.

With the situation worsening in Greece, many of the Greek royal family left Athens in a British Sunderland flying boat on 22 April. A day later, King George followed, heading for safety on Crete, only to be greeted by German air raids. The British Royal Navy destroyer HMS *Decoy* took the Greek royal family to join the Greek community in Egypt. However, following the fall of Crete, it was decided to evacuate the Greek royal exiles, Greek prime minister and his Cabinet to South Africa, and preparations were made ready for this on the *Nieuw Amsterdam.* Under a veil of secrecy and high security, the royal party and their entourage joined the ship at Suez on 27 June. Also on board for the voyage south were 151 other passengers, 5 naval personnel, 1,000 prisoners of war and their 75 escort guards.

The Dutch crew welcomed the royal visitors aboard the *Nieuw Amsterdam* in great reverence and they were provided with cabins and meals almost equal to peacetime standards. The Greek royal family – King George II, Crown Prince Paul, Crown Princess Frederika and their two children their Royal Highnesses Princess Sophia and Prince Constantine – were all deeply moved by the welcome they received aboard the *Nieuw Amsterdam.* The troopship was met by the heavy cruiser HMS *Cornwall* on 3 July to escort her into port as an enemy surface unit had been detected within 60 miles. On arrival in Durban on 7 July, special awards were presented by King George II to the senior Dutch officers of the crew of the *Nieuw Amsterdam* in recognition of the safety and comfort provided during the voyage to Durban. Commodore Bijl was created a commander in the Royal Order of the Phoenix, Staff Captain Rens Brandsand and Chief Engineer A.A. J Haman were decorated with Greece's Gold Cross in the Order of the Phoenix, purser Menno K Ziessen was awarded with the Silver Cross of the Royal Order of the Phoenix for their role in the Greek royal family's escape from Egypt. Later, Captain Rens Brandsand recalled in his memories of the voyage that, 'Crown Prince Paul was very nice and Princess Frederika was a darling'.

From 7 to 10 July the ship entered the dry docks in Durban for repair. The brief stay over in South Africa provided the crew with a short, much-needed rest and recuperation time and opportunity to relax on the famous Durban beaches. After release from the dry dock, the *Nieuw Amsterdam* joined the *Mauretania* and the *Ile de France* to form Convoy WS9A2 and was escorted by the cruiser *Cornwall* as far as Perim, where the ships dispersed as independents on 18 July. Their arrival in Suez was staggered to avoid congestion, with *Mauretania* and *Ile de France* docking on 21 July, followed by *Nieuw Amsterdam* on 23 July.

As the sun was rising in the early hours of daybreak on 23 July, the *Nieuw Amsterdam*, *Mauretania* and *Ile de France* rested peacefully at anchor in Suez preparing to sail to Durban in Convoy WS 9A2. Suddenly and without warning an air-raid siren sounded whilst troops were embarking. Rens Brands recalled:

> Sleeping gun crews quickly scrambled from their bunks as the sound of action stations aroused all three troopships. Within minutes the menacing drone of Luftwaffe Dornier and Heinkel aircraft could be discerned followed by a series of loud explosions as bombs rained down on the port. Guns from all three of our troopships targeted the skies. Luckily no casualties were reported, but many civilian properties were bombed in the densely populated Egyptian port. The warning of a threat of future bombing was heard loud and clear and all haste was made to sail from Suez the following day on 24 July.

For the next few months the *Nieuw Amsterdam* was assigned to working from Durban in South Africa and Aden at the foot of the Suez Canal on the Ministry of Defence officially designated 'CM convoy' route. On the next two voyages she travelled alone, carrying South African and Rhodesian troops outward and returning with Italian and German prisoners of war, sailing from Suez on 24 July, returning to Durban on 3 August, sailing again to Suez on 12 August, arriving at Suez on 24 August. For the voyage back to Durban from Suez on 25 August, the *Nieuw Amsterdam* joined Convoy CM15 which travelled at a slower speed, arriving in Durban on 4 September. The shuttle of troops from Durban continued with a solo voyage, sailing on 8 September and arriving in Suez on 20 September. During this voyage the ship encountered bad weather with unusually high waves. Those on board the *Nieuw Amsterdam* recalled encountering the infamous 'hole in the sea', where the ship descended into a double trough. This alarmed all those on board as the great Dutch liner at first dropped down between the wave pattern, as normal. However, instead of rising again, the liner dropped down at a steep angle into another unexpected trough. A mountainous wall of an enormous wave cascaded down from high above the ship and for a moment it was completely engulfed by water. Somehow the air within the ship created sufficient buoyancy to raise her, but the experience frightened all on board.

Returning from Suez on 21 September, the *Nieuw Amsterdam* once again joined the slow southbound convoy CM18 on 24 September at Aden, arriving off Durban on 31 September, but not docking until the following morning of 1 October. When the prisoners of war had disembarked, the ship was thoroughly inspected and examined for storm damage and repair assessment. Reluctantly, it was decided to withdraw the *Nieuw Amsterdam* from service while she awaited her turn in the queue to enter the dry dock for an intermediate refit to effect repairs. Work commenced in the dry dock in Durban on 30 October and was completed on 7 November. The work included a full boiler re-tube, replacement of propeller blades and a repaint, including the hull of the ship which had all barnacles removed. Steam had gradually been raised to full working pressure in the boilers on 6 November and the *Nieuw Amsterdam* was undocked the following morning to return to immediate service. Throughout the day of 8 November the Dutch troopship took on supplies of fuel, food and fresh water ready for sailing on the high tide with troops bound for the North African desert war. She was followed out of Durban by the *Nova Scotia* and the brace of ships joined northbound Convoy WS12. This convoy was escorted by the armed merchant cruiser *Cunnottar Castle*. The slow going convoy was joined by the battle cruiser Repulse which became the command escort until 14 November. This escort was relieved by the battleship HMS *Revenge* which took the convoy on to Aden where all ships dispersed on 19 November.

Following the intermediate refit, the ship was found to be a bit 'tight and stiff' at first when heading north, but she arrived safely at Aden on 19 November and continued her voyage to Suez on 22 November. She docked at Suez on 25 November and disembarkation of Allied troops commenced rapidly, with more captured Italian and North Afrika Korps POWs boarding the ship. Early on 27 November, the *Nieuw Amsterdam* returned solo to Durban maintaining a constant high speed throughout, docking back in Durban on 7 December.

The Christmas voyage from Durban commenced on Christmas Eve as part of Convoy WS 12ZA escorted by the cruiser Columbo. Three other vessels were in this convoy: *Aronda, Eastern Prince* and *Orduna*. A deck carol service was held aboard the *Nieuw Amsterdam* on Christmas Day morning and extra rations of rum were provided to the troops, with officers maintaining the traditional army custom of serving the lower ranks. The morale on board the *Nieuw Amsterdam* was said to be high as the New Year celebrations welcomed in 1942.

1942

The *Nieuw Amsterdam* arrived off Aden early on 4 January where the ships of Convoy WS 12ZA dispersed. The Dutch troop ship did not linger at Aden and sailed before sunrise the following morning, bound for Suez, where she arrived on 8 January. The return voyage from Suez, sailing on 11 January, was beset with boiler problems. Consequently, the *Nieuw Amsterdam* travelled at a reduced speed and limped into Durban on 21 January. After disembarking the consignment of POWs the ship waited her turn in the queue while the fireboxes cooled. Working around the clock, boiler repairs with tube replacements and new brick arches commenced on 26 January and were completed four days later on 30 January. After steam testing, the *Nieuw Amsterdam* was returned to service and sailed north with troop reinforcements for the North African campaign to Mombassa, where she called on 4 February. From here the ship sailed at speed to Aden, arriving on 8 February, and onwards to Suez, where she docked on 11 February.

Sailing from Suez on 12 February, the *Nieuw Amsterdam* headed east to Bombay in India, where she arrived on 19 February. Waiting on the quayside were the crack Sikh Rifle Brigade. These Indian soldiers were required to bolster the Axis advance towards Tobruk. The ship sailed on 24 February from Bombay, but returned for another shuttle voyage of reserve troops for Tobruk on 6 March. The high-speed dash must have taken its toll on the *Nieuw Amsterdam's* engines as, after depositing the Allied troops in Aden, she was forced to return to Durban for urgent repairs to the engines arriving on 28 March. The log records that the engine repairs commenced on 31 March, and following repair the ship was readied to sail north with more troop reinforcements on 6 April.

The devastating news of the fall of Tobruk and the advance of General Erwin Rommel's German Afrika Korps was met with disbelief on board the *Nieuw Amsterdam*. The British Eighth Army now fell back but was joined by fresh troops from the United States, which had entered the war the year before. From April until October 1942, the *Nieuw Amsterdam* was commanded by the British General Bernard Montgomery to undertake an intensive shuttle service between South Africa and Suez in order to build up troop reserves ready for the Battle of El Alamein, which took place from 23 October to 11 November.

In November 1942 Commodore Johannes Jacobus Bijl, who had taken the *Nieuw Amsterdam* on her maiden voyage and had since been her master, retired from service. In recognition of Commodore Bijl's distinguished service he was created an officer in the Order of Orange Nassau and Chief Engineer Haman was made a knight in the Order. Captain Barendse succeeded Commodore Bijl as master of the *Nieuw Amsterdam*.

On 22 November a Polish Special Unit of sixty soldiers boarded the *Nieuw Amsterdam.* Eight days later, anchoring at the port of Diego Suarez in Madagascar at 18 degrees south, 49 degrees east on 1 December, the Dutch crew on the ship watched as South African troops returning home embarked. They had been engaged in recent action with the British to liberate the island of Madagascar from Vichy French administration. This bay was said by many on board the *Nieuw Amsterdam* to be the most beautiful place the ship ever visited.

The South African soldiers began to haul up boxes and crates with what they said were 'souvenirs' to take home from the mangrove forests. No one suspected what was in those boxes and crates, but after the ship got underway all was soon revealed. Inside the boxes were exotic Mascarene parrots, fruit-eating bats, and huge tree boa and leaf-nosed snakes. The live cargo of souvenirs came to light when a South African soldier took a box up on the promenade deck and opened it. Before he could do anything, out jumped like a jack-in-the-box a Madagascar lemur monkey, closely followed by a second and third! The monkeys seized their apparent freedom and sprinted along the wooden deck to the front of the ship. Once here they began to climb. News of the escape soon spread around the ship and there were Dutch sailors, Polish Special Forces and South African running in all directions to apprehend the monkeys. Eventually they were cornered on the roof of the bridge, but could not be tempted down. The captain by this time was becoming very annoyed at the situation and ordered nets to be thrown over to recapture the absconders. Next, officers were dispatched below to inspect the souvenir boxes, which were kept under close guard until arrival at Durban on the morning of 7 December. The captain's orders were that before any of the human passengers disembarked the live souvenirs from Madagascar were to be first down the gangplank and off his ship!

The *Nieuw Amsterdam* continued to operate in the Pacific throughout the remainder of 1942 and into early 1943.

1943

On 10 March the *Nieuw Amsterdam* sailed from Wellington, New Zealand for San Francisco. She arrived on 22 March, passing under the famous Golden Gate Bridge. Here the Dutch flagship entered dry dock for a major refit to increase her troop-carrying capacity to 6,070 with standees being replaced by wooden bunks. All boilers were completely re-tubed and replacement of some firebox crown stays was undertaken and all brick arches renewed. The propellers were replaced and internal reinforcement patch plating added. The ship was given a complete repaint internally and externally. The British Ministry of Defence logbook records that the hydraulic and steam testing of the boilers was certified in late April and the ship prepared for sailing from San Francisco on 3 May. She arrived back in Wellington for an overnight stay on 16 May and sailed the next morning to Fremantle, arriving on 24 May. She resumed her shuttle duties from New Zealand, Australia and South Africa transporting Commonwealth troops to Suez until early October 1943.

One notable voyage during the summer of 1943 was the sailing from Wellington on 11 July, arriving at Port Tewfik on 18 August. The *Nieuw Amsterdam* carried 6,000 men of the 10th Maori 2nd New Zealand Expeditionary Force. The ship was said to be a place of 'great joy, singing and happiness' during this voyage. There are records of deck concerts, games and much festivity – most unlike any other wartime voyage.

Far left: A huge crowd of families and friends of departing New Zealand troops wave their fond farewells to loved ones on the decks of the *Nieuw Amsterdam*, which is shown sailing from Wellington during the Second World War. (Charles P. S. Boyer/ National Library of New Zealand)

Left: New Zealand troops are pictured on the deck of the *Nieuw Amsterdam* playing deck quoits during the Second World War. (National Library of New Zealand)

Left: New Zealand troops receive instruction on map reading on the deck of the troopship *Nieuw Amsterdam* during the Second World War. (National Library of New Zealand)

In September 1943 at a meeting in Whitehall, the future deployment of all troopships was discussed in depth and plans formulated for requirements for troop concentrations for Operation Overload and the invasion of Europe in 1944. The Admiralty decided that the *Nieuw Amsterdam* would sail from Wellington on 4 October to return to the dry dock in San Francisco for her second refit of the year. The troop-carrying capacity was to be further extended with alterations to accommodate 8,065 troops. This time the US Navy was fully prepared and the *Nieuw Amsterdam* arrived late on 15 October and immediately entered the shipyard at San Francisco early on the morning of 16 October. With great efficiency, working around the clock, the conversion was complete ready for the ship to return to service on 1 November.

Joining the *Nieuw Amsterdam* at San Francisco were members of the United States 312th Division. These 7,000 American GIs crammed aboard the ship bound for Sydney. Officers slept in the state rooms and the enlisted men slept where they could: on deck, below in hammocks or on mattresses. The indoor first-class swimming pool was even converted into sleeping quarters. Here sixty-four GIs slept in standee bunks five high! The junior officers slept up to four in a cabin, senior officers two to a suite, and only the senior commanding officers would have their own cabin. Life in this claustrophobic environment consisted of two meals a day, news broadcasts, playing poker, reading and self entertainment with musical activities, deck concerts and boxing matches. There were occasional lifeboat drills and many heated arguments! For the lifeboat drill aboard the *Nieuw Amsterdam* each man was given a life preserver to wear which was equipped with a small battery operated light on it. Troops would gaze at the lifeboats and wonder if there was enough capacity to take all on board.

The great Dutch troopship set out on her final Pacific voyage arriving in Wellington on 6 November. During her stay in Wellington, the prime minister of New Zealand, the Hon. Peter Frazer, and fourteen members of the New Zealand cabinet came on board the *Nieuw Amsterdam*. They were very impressed by the courtesy of the Dutch officers and crew and expressed their sincere thanks to all for the safe passage of New Zealand troops that had been carried aboard. The *Nieuw Amsterdam* sailed from Wellington on 15 November watched by an enthusiastic crowd bound for Sydney. Here she stayed overnight on 19–20 November, returning for a farewell visit to Wellington on 22–24 November. She now set sail on her long voyage home to the North Atlantic from San Francisco on 8 December, calling at Los Angeles on 15 December and San Pedro on 17 December.

1944

The voyage home to the North Atlantic continued with visits to Auckland on 18 January, Durban on 20 February, Cape Town on 22 February and Freetown from 29 February to 2 March. Sailing from Freetown the mood on board the *Nieuw Amsterdam* changed with the worry of the threat of German U-boat torpedo attack. Extra lookouts were stationed around the ship to scour the seas through binoculars. The ship increased speed following an unpredictable zigzag path in order to outrun the lurking menace beneath the waves. As the ship entered the Western Approaches, the sight of a circling Coastal Command Air Speed Oxford sent a feeling of reassurance and celebration through the *Nieuw Amsterdam*, which was followed by loud cheers and waves. Arriving back in the cold Clyde on 12 March, the reality of being back in home waters began to sink in. Here a new crew joined the ship ready to sail from the Clyde across the choppy North Atlantic on 15 March as part of Convoy TA97B to Halifax.

In April 1944 a telegram was received with news for the master of the *Nieuw Amsterdam*, Captain Barendse, who was appointed as commodore of the fleet. By this time he had been serving the company for forty-one years.

A superb aerial view of the *Nieuw Amsterdam* when serving as a troopship, taken on 18 April 1944. She is painted in her drab wartime all over grey livery. (Ernest Arroyo Collection)

From 7 to 31 May the *Nieuw Amsterdam* underwent a major refit in the dry dock at Todd's Shipyard. Whilst in Hoboken, the ship received an unofficial visit from Her Royal Highness Princess Juliana. She was welcomed aboard by Commodore George J. Barendse, who introduced the officers and crew to her during the tour of the ship. The visit concluded with a small buffet luncheon in the former children's playroom on the upper promenade deck. The effect of this royal visit was to lift the morale of all on board and make them feel just how valued and appreciated their contribution to the war effort was.

If the conditions aboard the *Nieuw Amsterdam* felt cramped whilst conveying troops in the Pacific, they were sheer luxury compared to what was to follow in the lead up to D-Day and the invasion of Europe in June 1944. American GIs were frequently packed 500 at a time into rooms located at the bow of the ship that had been converted from the peacetime on-board cinema. One GI named Joe Bernal commented: 'We're packed in like sardines.' Another GI responded: 'Yeah, everything but the oil.' Not only was the space for each GI small, but they also had to stow all their gear in the bunk with them. This included a steel helmet, gas mask, backpack, duffel bag, overcoat and blankets. Some GIs kept their rifles in their bunks, but the majority of men hung them up from the pipe frame of the bed. This had the knock-on effect of producing an obstacle to scramble past.

The brave American GIs heading to Europe were confined to quarters except to go to the latrine, eat and for limited exercise up on deck when the Atlantic seas and weather permitted. When Atlantic storms brewed and the *Nieuw Amsterdam* tossed and rolled in the waves it had a devastating effect on those below. There would be much vomiting with nowhere for it to go but on the floor beside the bunks. The sleeping quarters were hot, smelly places lacking oxygen and peace and quiet, as men were constantly snoring, muttering, talking and arguing. There was no ship store or library and the troops had to exchange magazines and books, but even so the light in the quarters was very poor. Some men spent the time at sea writing letters to loved ones, which would be read and censored before reaching their final destinations.

The toilet facilities were a latrine, which was just a basic galvanised steel trough. These were frequently clogged up from men vomiting in them and the rolling of the ship would cause them to spill over onto the floor. The mess hall on board the *Nieuw Amsterdam* was another disastrous location. The two meals served per day were in five sittings. Colour coded cards were distributed to the troops in their quarters, which were given to the ship's police on entering the mess hall at the appointed time of each sitting. Food was served cafeteria-style and the troops ate using their own mess kits. No chairs were provided to sit on in the mess hall. Instead the troops stood at chest high wooden tables, which were bolted to the floor. In bad weather, when the vessel swayed from side to side, eating whilst standing became chaotic and food often cascaded onto the floor.

Brave American GIs bound for the European theatre of war are entertained on the deck of the troopship *Nieuw Amsterdam* with a concert and jive dancing. (Associated Press)

Food preparation on board the *Nieuw Amsterdam* was supervised by British crew with Dutch cooks. West Indian conscripts did all kitchen cleaning duties and basic food preparation. Breakfast usually consisted of lumpy oatmeal porridge or something that the American GIs nicknamed 'SOS' (shit on a shingle) which was a mixture of minced meat and powdered milk on toast, frequently served burnt. This culinary delight was greasy, unpalatable yellow glob! Extra powdered milk was available for the brave – it was described by many as liquid chalk. The second meal of the day aboard the *Nieuw Amsterdam* was usually Spam sandwiches or boiled beef stew served with boiled vegetables, which on occasion included a boiled caterpillar or grub. The North Atlantic voyage menu on

Above: This picture gives some indication of the cramped conditions on board the troop ship *Nieuw Amsterdam* which is packed with American GIs and their equipment as they sail across the Atlantic in 1944. (Associated Press)

Above: The Hollywood screen icon, Jane Russell, was recruited by the US Navy to assist with a publicity campaign. She is pictured on the deck of the troopship *Nieuw Amsterdam* promoting a poster, 'A slip of the lip may sink a ship'. After refurbishment of the ship after the Second World War, the actress Jane Russell was a regular passenger on her favourite classic liner when travelling across the Atlantic. (Associated Press)

Left: The troopship *Nieuw Amsterdam* is overflowing with soldiers who are gazing from every vantage point on the decks. (Britton Collection)

the *Nieuw Amsterdam* was thus something to be endured and GIs counted down each serving to landfall. The daily quantities of food consumed on the *Nieuw Amsterdam* at this time were quite staggering. Each day the kitchens prepared 240 gallons of powdered milk, 80 bags of flour, 1,110 dozen eggs, 1,000lb of bacon, 6,400 quarts of coffee, 1,100lb of cold cuts, 14,000 loaves of bread and 880lb of butter. When beef stew was served it required 22 hinds of beef, for lamb stew 110 carcasses and for boiled brisket of beef 4,000lb were required.

During the build up to D-Day in 1944 the *Nieuw Amsterdam* managed to cross the Atlantic with three round-trip voyages. However, further voyages were interrupted by the need for repair at Todd's Shipyard in

New York between 7 and 31 May. The ship re-entered service on 3 June and sailed from New York as a member of Convoy AT121. She returned westwards across the Atlantic as a member of Convoy TA121 to Halifax. By this time Atlantic convoys were receiving almost continuous air support from long range Liberator and Coastal Command Short Sunderland aircraft. Surface patrol vessels were now equipped with better radar and sonar sets, which greatly reduced the German U-boat menace. The secret Enigma code used to transmit orders to U-boat wolf packs had been broken by the Allies and all intercepted messages were relayed via Bletchley Park to Atlantic convoys.

On 4 August the *Nieuw Amsterdam* took a break from the North Atlantic and sailed south, calling briefly at Freetown on 13 August before heading onwards south to Cape Town where she arrived on 22 August. According to the logbook her stay in Cape Town appears to have been very brief and after refuelling and replenishing food and fresh water the *Nieuw Amsterdam* made a same-day return. Amongst the food supplies were an abundant fresh supply of Cape oranges and apples. After calling in overnight at Freetown on 3–4 September, the ship continued north, returning to Greenock on 13 September. The reason for this unusual, very brief and high-speed voyage to the South Atlantic remains a mystery, and is listed by HM Government with a 'D Notice official secret – strictly not for publication' to this day.

Upon return to the North Atlantic the *Nieuw Amsterdam* recommenced her shuttle operations of troops from the USA and Canada to Britain. Sailing from Gourock on 18 December, the *Nieuw Amsterdam* sailed once again north-west across the Atlantic, bound for Halifax, with 2,284 troops on board. The British destroyer escorts broke away at daybreak on 19 December to return to the Clyde. Off the coast of Nova Scotia in the late morning of Christmas Day a Canadian escort aircraft rendezvoused with the ship, circling above. Approximately one and half hours before embarking the harbour pilot for Halifax, the pilot of the aircraft spotted a lurking German U-boat at periscope depth hidden under the surface of the waves ready to torpedo the ship. The Canadian aircraft pilot did not have time to transmit his message in code and transmitted in plain language to the HMT *Nieuw Amsterdam:* 'Hard starboard. Ram a German U-boat!' On board the ship, action stations were sounded and gunnery crews sprinted to their stations. Meanwhile the *Nieuw Amsterdam* swiftly altered course to starboard. Realising that it had been spotted, the submarine dived and the two vessels narrowly missed each other.

Submerging beneath the waves was *Kriegsmarine U-806* under the command of Captain Hornbostel. As Allied destroyers approached the U-boat rested silently on the bottom of the Halifax Approaches for twenty-one hours as the escorts passed overhead randomly dropping depth charges. According to Chief Officer Cornelis 'Kees' Haagmans, sailing on the *Nieuw Amsterdam,* it was a narrow escape.

1945

The crew of the ship celebrated the New Year of 1945 with great optimism to an end to the war in Europe in the hotels and bars of Halifax in style and the ship sailed on 3 January 1945 with 6,293 Canadian troops bound for the Clyde. Hidden and waiting beneath the waves were three U-boats: *U-806* commanded by Captain Hornbostel, *U-231* commanded by Captain Lessing and *U-1232* commanded by Captain Dobratz. The *U-1232* had been the last U-boat to reach the Nova Scotia area in December 1944. Her 40-year-old captain, Kurt Dobratz, sailed from Norway on 12 November 1944. He was a one-time Luftwaffe pilot with a great sense of humour. He challenged the two other U-boat captains in a contest to 'outdo them'. Waiting to pounce beneath the surface on the morning of 3 January he spotted through his periscope a T-S destroyer escort and the great prize of the HMT *Nieuw Amsterdam* sailing just behind the escort. As the rich Allied troopship quarry sailed towards *U-1232*, Captain Dobratz, according to his diaries, fired off one torpedo at the escort destroyer and three further torpedoes at the *Nieuw Amsterdam.* Happily for those on board the troopship all three torpedoes missed their target and exploded in the wake of the ship! The ship increased speed and zigzagged to outrun and outmanoeuvre the U-boat pursuers beneath the waves.

Arriving at the Clyde via the Northern Entrance on 9 January, there was great relief aboard the *Nieuw Amsterdam.* After a quick turn around, the ship was ready to sail to New York with 1,946 US troops on 14 January. Arriving at New York on 22 January, the ship set sail again on 28 January north bound for Halifax, where she was escorted in to counter any U-boat threat. Here 6,801 Canadians embarked heading for Europe ready for the conclusion of the war against Germany. Again the ship was escorted out of Halifax into the North Atlantic by a destroyer, which stayed close to the troopship for 14 hours before breaking off.

The ship sailed again from the Clyde on 14 February as part of Convoy TA186, carrying 3,115 Canadian troops, of which 453 were wounded men. During the crossing the *Nieuw Amsterdam* encountered some severe weather conditions with oncoming high winds resulting in 60ft waves. With speed consequently reduced, the arrival in Halifax was delayed until the afternoon of 21 February. On the evening before the Canadian troops were in high spirits about their homecoming. The thirty-seven watertight doors on the ship were always closed during sailing, and they could be centrally locked from the bridge when required. This meant that one had to go to a higher deck when going from one section to another in the lower parts of the ship. The log records an unfortunate and fatal incident involving one of the Canadian soldiers returning from Europe. He decided to take a shortcut when returning to his sleeping quarters; instead of going up via the upper promenade deck, he opened a heavy watertight door on the main deck by hand. When the door had sufficiently opened enough so that he could scramble through, the soldier let go of the handle; however, before he could fully pass through the gap the heavy door closed again. Sadly, the unsuspecting soldier was killed just hours before being reunited with his loved ones.

On 26 February the *Nieuw Amsterdam* sailed from Halifax with 6,841 troops aboard and was escorted by two destroyers for the first twelve hours of the voyage. She sailed at high speed, following a zigzag course, and arrived safely in Liverpool on 4 March. The ship departed again, sailing from Liverpool on 8 March with 1,803 US GIs, of whom 647 were wounded. The ship was part of Convoy AT201 bound for New York and was escorted throughout by two destroyers. After the ship was docked at Hoboken on 16 March and the troops were disembarked, shore leave was granted for the crew.

With the war in Europe now nearing its conclusion in the spring of 1945, the Admiralty agreed to send the *Nieuw Amsterdam* to Todd's Shipyard in New York for refit in preparation for future service in the Pacific. The aim was to use the *Nieuw Amsterdam* as a troop transport to help defeat the Japanese. She entered Todd's dry dock on 16 March. Here the ship's heavy gun and the stabilisation slabs it was mounted upon were removed. The ballast in hold 4 was also removed before the ship was released on 5 April following boiler and engine repairs. She remerged rejuvenated and set sail from Hoboken on 7 April with 5,695 US troops and a party of Dutch VIP civilian passengers bound for the Clyde. Unusually the *Nieuw Amsterdam* approached from the south-west and was escorted north through the Irish Sea with surface escort and Coastal Command air cover, arriving at the Clyde on 16 April.

After disembarking the US GIs the ship welcomed on board 4,447 rowdy and excitable Australian troops who were returning home plus twenty-nine US gunners for the Nieuw Amsterdam's anti-aircraft guns. Last to come aboard the ship were 180 Wrens under the command of Lt Commander Irene Farqueharson, all of whom received wolf whistles and loud cheers from the Australians lining the decks. Lt Commander Farqueharson was said to be 'not amused' and her first action aboard was to complain to the Australian CO and instruct him to keep his soldiers under control. The *Nieuw Amsterdam* set sail on 22 April and passed Gibraltar on 27 April heading into the Mediterranean. She passed Port Said on 1 May, passing through the Suez Canal and sailed from Suez on 4 May. On 8 May 1945 news reached the *Nieuw Amsterdam* that the Germans had surrendered unconditionally in Europe. This was greeted with huge celebrations by all on board. Servings of Royal Navy rum and US beers flowed and a few flares were fired off in the absence of fireworks! The crew of the *Nieuw Amsterdam* received two days' extra pay plus two days' leave in lieu.

The *Nieuw Amsterdam* was now back in familiar old territory and sailed to Fremantle calling to refuel and disembark part of the Australian troops from 16 to 18 May, before resuming the voyage to Sydney arriving on 21 May with returning exhausted but exuberant Australian and New Zealand troops. Newsreels shot at Sydney Woolloomooloo Pier show cheering troops lining the decks and climbing the masts for a first sight of loved ones waiting on the quayside. When the ship had been cleared, the crew were granted their two days shore leave to celebrate VE Day. Commodore George J. Barendse and Chief Officer Cornelis 'Kees' Haagmans were invited ashore to join the official celebrations and had lunch with Admiral Sir Bruce Fraser. The skeleton crew who remained on board received several crates of chilled Australian beers and Australian wines to have as part of the festivities.

The return voyage to Liverpool was made at a leisurely pace owing to a failure of a boiler, via Durban (15–19 June), Cape Town (21–22 June) and Freetown (29–30 June). Arriving at Liverpool on 6 July, it was determined that the *Nieuw Amsterdam* should not go to Birkenhead in England for repairs, but should sail to Halifax on 18 July with returning Canadian troops and thence onwards to New York for repair. She arrived in New York on 26 July and repairs were completed by 11 August.

Sailing from Hoboken Pier in New York on 24 August with 507 passengers and 200 children, the *Nieuw Amsterdam* headed east across the Atlantic to Southampton where she docked for the first time since before the outbreak of war on 31 August. Whilst in port on 2 September the news came through that the Japanese had surrendered. Along with the other ships docked in the Port of Southampton, the *Nieuw Amsterdam* blew her whistle several times in celebration of the end of the Second World War. The Dutch and British crew aboard celebrated the news with liberal helpings of alcohol, following by much singing and dancing on the decks.

During the stay over in Southampton all of the armour aboard the ship was removed and transferred ashore. The *Nieuw Amsterdam* was now put to work on two voyages returning Canadian and US GIs troops from Europe to Halifax. On 4 September the ship sailed from Southampton with 7,718 Canadian troops and some VIPs of various Dutch steamship companies. Arriving in Halifax on 9 September and sailing again on 13 September with 1,530 Canadians and 196 German POWs to Southampton. After docking at Southampton on 19 September, several of the officers of the *Nieuw Amsterdam* decided to return home to Holland for the first time since 1939. Meanwhile, the ship sailed from Southampton again on 24 September with 7,714 Canadians, arriving in Halifax on 29 October.

Returning to Southampton on 8 October, she underwent engine repairs with assistance from Vosper Thorneycroft engineers. On 10 October, the *Nieuw Amsterdam* was returned from Cunard White Star Line management to the Holland America Line. The Dutch house flag was proudly raised high and tears ran down the cheeks of many of the Dutch officers and crew as the flag fluttered in the breeze from the mast. Following on from the flag ceremony a formal lunch was served on board the *Nieuw Amsterdam* to the VIPs of both Cunard and Holland America Lines and a champagne toast was raised to salute the ship.

On 28 October with the Holland America Line proudly flying above the *Nieuw Amsterdam* sailed from Southampton with 4,722 Dutch troops and 203 female members of the Dutch Navy and Army bound for Trincomali on the east coast of Ceylon. Here 200 more people and 50 Red Cross staff were embarked on 14 October. The ship arrived in Penang on 16 October where 2,200 troops disembarked. The *Nieuw Amsterdam* resumed her voyage on 18 October heading for Port Sweetenham, but a last-minute message received on board informed the captain not to disembark the troops here, but to proceed 130 miles to Port Dickson and disembark the remaining Dutch troops there. Between Port Sweetenham and Port Dickson, the records show that a Dutch soldier jumped overboard. The ship immediately stopped engines and circled. He was spotted in the water and a motor boat was lowered to rescue him. After safe return to the ship, the soldier was sent to the ship's hospital with nervous exhaustion from battle fatigue.

The ship now set out to return home but when she reached Gibraltar on 30 October, an urgent message was received to divert to the Dutch East Indies. The *Nieuw Amsterdam* doubled back, returning to Port Said on 3 November and straight through the Suez Canal reaching Suez the next day. From here the ship sailed at speed to Trincomali, where she anchored off on 13–14 November. A tender boat was sent ashore and shuttled Dutch evacuees back to the Nieuw Amsterdam. From here the ship sailed unplanned to Port Swettenham, Pennang arriving on 17 November, then straight on to Port Dickson on 20 November and Singapore on 22 November. The ship remained on standby at Singapore and over the next few days she was thoroughly cleaned. Sailing from Singapore on 8 December, with 4,450 repatriated citizens from the Dutch East Indies, including 2,000 widows with their children from Japanese concentration camps, the ship briefly called at Cochim on 12–13 December to collect further evacuees and 730 British troops. Arriving at Suez on 20 December to refuel and take on fresh water and supplies, the ship sailed on Christmas Eve through the Suez Canal. Passing Port Said on Christmas Day 1945, she met up with another Holland America Line ship, the *Volendam*, which was also loaded with evacuees from Java. The pair of Dutch ships travelled together through the Mediterranean, passing Gibraltar on 29 December.

1946

They celebrated the New Year at the Nab Tower off Bembridge on the Isle of Wight whilst waiting for the pilot through the Solent. Both ships are

Local pleasure craft steamed out enthusiastically from Rotterdam to meet the returning *Nieuw Amsterdam* on 10 April 1946. Her funnels were painted in the Holland America Line house colours and she was dressed all over for the occasion. (Courtesy of Piet van Dijk, World Ship Society, Netherlands)

Although looking rusted and neglected through years of service as a troopship during the Second World War, the *Nieuw Amsterdam* returned home to Rotterdam on 10 April 1946. Her funnels were painted in the Holland America Line house colours and she was dressed all over for the occasion. (Gordon Turner/Britton Collection)

recorded as docking in Southampton at 9.30 a.m. on 1 January where they were met by representatives of the Netherlands Consulate and members of the Red Cross. Via two Dutch passenger ships the Dutch passengers sailed from Southampton the next day to Rotterdam.

The ship's log records the words: 'EDC not working. Transfer to King George V Graving Dock.' Here the *Nieuw Amsterdam* remained until 22 January during which time her funnels were repainted in Holland America Line livery. This said, the *Nieuw Amsterdam* remained under British management and sailed from Southampton on 25 January for a final return voyage to Singapore. The log records that she passed Malta on 29 January, Port Said on 1 February, Suez on 2 February, Aden on 5 February, Colombo on 10 and 11 February and arrived at Singapore on 15 February. After collecting more evacuees from Java, she returned from Singapore on 16 March docking in Southampton docking at 12.55 p.m. on 8 April. The remaining members of the British crew disembarked at 2.30 p.m. and the *Nieuw Amsterdam* became an all Dutch crew for the first time since the outbreak of the Second World War. After refuelling, the next day she prepared to weigh anchor and sail home to Rotterdam. The logbook records, written in red ink: 'Released from STA1 30.4.46. Redelivering to Dutch at Rotterdam effective from 8.4.46.'

In the course of the Second World War, the *Nieuw Amsterdam* transported 378,361 troops and passengers and sailed 530,452 nautical miles across the oceans of the world, a distance equivalent to almost twenty-one times around the Earth's circumference. The *Nieuw Amsterdam* and the other Allied troopship liners shortened the length of the war by up to two years according to the British wartime Prime Minister Winston Churchill. The enormous contribution of the *Nieuw Amsterdam* must also take into account that Dutch citizens from the Dutch East Indies were repatriated to the Netherlands. Without doubt the *Nieuw Amsterdam* was an unsung hero of the Second World War.

Summary of Wartime Movements Between Ports:

12/09/1940 New York 13/09/1940 Halifax 1 29 Halifax Canada For conversion at Halifax to troop-carrying operations
26/10/1940 Cape Town 08/11/1940 Singapore 14 20 Singapore
10/11/1940 Halifax 25/10/1940 Cape Town 15 1 Cape Town South Africa
24/12/1940 Singapore 03/01/1941 Sydney 11 20 Sydney Australia
23/01/1941 Sydney 27/01/1941 Wellington 4 4 Wellington New Zealand
01/02/1941 Wellington 04/02/1941 Sydney 3 1 Sydney Australia
04/02/1941 Sydney 10/02/1941 Fremantle 6 2 Fremantle Australia
12/02/1941 Fremantle 22/02/1941 Bombay 10 5 Bombay India
27/02/1941 Bombay 01/03/1941 Colombo 2 7 Colombo Ceylon (Sri Lanka)
08/03/1941 Colombo 15/03/1941 Fremantle 7 2 Fremantle Australia
17/03/1941 Fremantle 22/03/1941 Sydney 5 6 Sydney Australia
28/03/1941 Sydney 31/03/194 Wellington 3 7 Wellington New Zealand
07/04/1941 Wellington 10/04/1941 Sydney 3 1 Sydney Australia
11/04/1941 Sydney 16/04/1941 Fremantle 5 3 Fremantle Australia
19/04/1941 Fremantle 29/04/1941 Singapore 10 9 Singapore Singapore Anzac troops to Singapore
08/05/1941 Singapore 15/05/1941 Bombay 7 3 Bombay India
18/05/1941 Bombay 23/05/1941 Mombasa 5 1 Mombasa Kenya
24/05/1941 Mombasa 28/05/1941 Durban 4 13 Durban South Africa
10/06/1941 Durban 20/06/1941 Suez 10 7 Suez Egypt North African Campaign Allied Trooping – SA & Anzac
27/06/1941 Suez 07/07/1941 Durban 10 4 Durban South Africa -

11/07/1941 Durban 23/07/1941 Suez 12 1 Suez Egypt North African Campaign Allied Trooping – SA & Anzac
24/07/1941 Suez 03/08/1941 Durban 10 8 Durban South Africa
11/08/1941 Durban 24/08/1941 Suez 13 1 Suez Egypt North African Campaign Allied Trooping – SA & Anzac
25/08/1941 Suez 05/09/1941 Durban 11 3 Durban South Africa
08/09/1941 Durban 20/09/1941 Suez 12 1 Suez Egypt North African Campaign Allied Trooping – SA & Anzac
21/09/1941 Suez 01/10/1941 Durban 11 7 Durban South Africa
08/11/1941 Durban 19/11/1941 Aden 9 3 Aden Aden Protectorate North African Campaign Allied Trooping – SA & Anzac
22/11/1941 Aden 25/11/1941 Suez 3 2 Suez Egypt North African Campaign Allied Trooping – SA & Anzac
27/11/1941 Suez 07/12/1941 Durban 15 16 Durban South Africa
23/12/1941 Durban 04/01/1942 Aden 11 1 Aden Aden Protectorate North African Campaign Allied Trooping – SA & Anzac
05/01/1942 Aden 09/01/1942 Suez 4 2 Suez Egypt North African Campaign Allied Trooping – SA & Anzac
11/01/1942 Suez 14/01/1942 Berbera 3 1 Berbera British Somaliland British Somaliland
14/01/1942 Berbera 21/01/1942 Durban 7 13 Durban South Africa
03/02/1942 Durban 04/02/1942 Mombasa 2 1 Mombasa Kenya North African Campaign Allied Trooping – SA
04/02/1942 Mombasa 08/02/1942 Aden 4 1 Aden Aden Protectorate North African Campaign Allied Trooping – SA & Anzac
08/02/1942 Aden 12/02/1942 Suez 4 1 Suez Egypt North African Campaign Allied Trooping – SA & Anzac
13/02/1942 Suez 19/02/1942 Bombay 6 5 Bombay India
24/02/1942 Bombay 28/02/1942 Aden 4 1 Aden Aden Protectorate North African Campaign Allied Trooping – Indian
28/02/1942 Aden 04/03/1942 Suez 4 2 Suez Egypt North African Campaign Allied Trooping – Indian
06/03/1942 Suez 09/03/1942 Aden 3 1 Aden Aden Protectorate North African Campaign Allied Trooping – SA & Anzac
09/03/1942 Aden 14/03/1942 Colombo 5 5 Colombo Ceylon (Sri Lanka)
19/03/1942 Colombo 27/03/1942 Durban 8 9 Durban South Africa
06/04/1942 Durban 16/04/1942 Suez 10 1 Suez Egypt North Africa Campaign Supply Transport – SA & Anzac
17/04/1942 Suez 28/04/1942 Durban 11 1 Durban South Africa German POW Transport
29/04/1942 Durban 01/05/1942 Cape Town 3 3 Cape Town South Africa German POW Transport
04/05/1942 Cape Town 05/05/1942 Simon's Town 1 2 Simon's Town South Africa Transfer Afrika Korps POWS to S.S. Queen Mary for Canadian POW Camps
07/05/1942 Simon's Town 07/05/1942 Cape Town 1 6 Cape Town South Africa
13/05/1942 Cape Town 25/05/1942 Suez 12 2 Suez Egypt North African Campaign Allied Trooping – SA & Anzac
27/05/1942 Suez 06/06/1942 Durban 10 2 Durban South Africa
07/06/1942 Durban 11/06/1942 Cape Town 4 2 Cape Town South Africa
13/06/1942 Cape Town 14/06/1942 Port Elizabeth 2 11 Port Elizabeth South Africa
25/06/1942 Port Elizabeth 26/06/1942 Durban 2 1 Durban South Africa
27/06/1942 Durban 09/07/1942 Suez 13 2 Suez Egypt
11/07/1942 Suez 22/07/1942 Durban 11 11 Durban South Africa
03/08/1942 Durban 08/08/1942 Diego Suarez 5 1 Diego Suarez Madagascar Madagascan Campaign Trooping – South Africa
09/08/1942 Diego Suarez 11/08/1942 Mombasa 2 1 Mombasa Kenya
12/08/1942 Mombasa 18/08/1942 Cape Town 6 3 Cape Town South Africa
21/08/1942 Cape Town 23/08/1942 Durban 3 1 Durban South Africa
24/08/1942 Durban 06/09/1942 Suez 13 1 Suez Egypt
07/09/1942 Suez 19/09/1942 Durban 12 10 Durban South Africa
29/09/1942 Durban 01/10/1942 Cape Town 3 2 Cape Town South Africa
03/10/1942 Cape Town 17/10/1942 Suez 14 2 Suez Egypt
19/10/1942 Suez 31/10/1942 Durban 12 8 Durban South Africa
07/11/1942 Durban 12/11/1942 Diego Suarez 5 1 Diego Suarez Madagascar Madagascan Campaign Trooping – SA
13/11/1942 Diego Suarez 17/11/1942 Aden 4 1 Aden Aden Protectorate
18/11/1942 Aden 21/11/1942 Suez 3 2 Suez Egypt
23/11/1942 Suez 01/12/1942 Diego Suarez 8 2 Diego Suarez Madagascar Madagascan Campaign Trooping – SA
03/12/1942 Diego Suarez 07/12/1942 Durban 4 13 Durban South Africa
20/12/1942 Durban 31/12/1942 Suez 11 3 Suez Egypt
02/01/1943 Suez 13/01/1943 Durban 11 6 Durban South Africa
19/01/1943 Durban 30/01/1943 Suez 11 2 Suez Egypt
01/02/1943 Suez 09/02/1943 Maldives 8 1 Maldives Indian Ocean Islands
10/02/1943 Maldives 18/02/1043 Fremantle 8 2 Fremantle Australia
20/02/1943 Fremantle 25/02/1943 Port Melbourne 5 9 Port Melbourne Australia
06/03/1943 Port Melbourne 10/03/1943 Wellington 4 1 Wellington New Zealand
10/03/1943 Wellington 22/03/1943 San Francisco 12 11 San Francisco USA
03/05/1943 San Francisco 16/05/1943 Wellington 13 2 Wellington New Zealand Pacific Campaign Trooping – USA
18/05/1943 Wellington 25/05/1943 Fremantle 7 1 Fremantle Australia

26/05/1943 Fremantle 04/06/1943 Colombo 9 1 Colombo Ceylon (Sri Lanka)
05/06/1943 Colombo 13/06/1943 Suez 8 2 Suez Egypt
15/06/1943 Suez 18/06/1943 Aden 3 2 Aden Aden Protectorate
20/06/1943 Aden 01/07/1943 Fremantle 11 2 Fremantle Australia
03/07/1943 Fremantle 08/07/1943 Hobart 5 1 Hobart Australia
08/07/1943 Hobart 12/07/1943 Wellington 4 11 Wellington New Zealand
23/07/1943 Wellington 27/07/1943 Hobart 4 1 Hobart Australia
27/07/1943 Hobart 02/08/1943 Fremantle 6 2 Fremantle Australia
04/08/1943 Fremantle 18/08/1943 Suez 14 4 Suez Egypt
22/08/1943 Suez 24/08/1943 Massawa 2 1 Massawa Eritrea
25/08/1943 Massawa 09/09/1943 Durban 15 1 Durban South Africa
10/09/1943 Durban 20/09/1943 Fremantle 10 3 Fremantle Australia
23/09/1943 Fremantle 26/09/1943 Port Melbourne 3 1 Port Melbourne Australia
27/09/1943 Port Melbourne 02/10/1943 Wellington 6 2 Wellington New Zealand
04/10/1943 Wellington 16/10/1943 San Francisco 12 16 San Francisco USA
01/11/1943 San Francisco 15/11/1943 Wellington 14 1 Wellington New Zealand Pacific Campaign Trooping – USA
16/11/1943 Wellington 19/11/1943 Sydney 3 2 Sydney Australia
21/11/1943 Sydney 24/11/1943 Wellington 3 1 Wellington New Zealand
25/11/1943 Wellington 07/12/1943 San Francisco 12 8 San Francisco USA
15/12/1943 San Francisco 16/12/1943 San Pedro 1 15 San Pedro USA
31/12/1943 San Pedro 01/01/1944 San Francisco 1 4 San Francisco USA
05/01/1944 San Francisco 18/01/1944 Auckland 13 1 Auckland New Zealand Pacific Campaign Trooping – USA
19/01/1944 Auckland 22/01/1944 Sydney 3 5 Sydney Australia
27/01/1944 Sydney 29/01/1944 Port Melbourne 2 1 Port Melbourne Australia
29/01/1944 Port Melbourne 10/02/1944 Durban 12 10 Durban South Africa
20/02/1944 Durban 22/02/1944 Cape Town 2 1 Cape Town South Africa
22/02/1944 Cape Town 29/02/1944 Freetown 7 2 Freetown Sierra Leone
02/03/1944 Freetown 12/03/1944 Gourock 10 3 Gourock Scotland
15/03/1944 Gourock 22/03/1944 Halifax 7 3 Halifax Canada
26/03/1944 Halifax 01/04/1944 Gourock 6 4 Gourock Scotland USA Troops to Europe prior to D-Day.
05/04/1944 Gourock 13/04/1944 New York 8 5 New York USA
18/04/1944 New York 26/04/1944 Gourock 8 3 Gourock Scotland USA Troops to Europe prior to D-Day.
29/04/1944 Gourock 07/05/1944 New York 9 27 New York USA
03/06/1944 New York 12/06/1944 Gourock 9 2 Gourock Scotland USA Troops to Europe
14/06/1944 Gourock 21/06/1944 Halifax 7 5 Halifax Canada
26/06/1944 Halifax 02/07/1944 Gourock 6 3 Gourock Scotland USA Troops to Europe
05/07/1944 Gourock 11/07/1944 Halifax 6 9 Halifax Canada
20/07/1944 Halifax 26/07/1944 Gourock 6 9 Gourock Scotland USA Troops to Europe
04/08/1944 Gourock 13/08/1944 Freetown 9 1 Freetown Sierra Leone
14/08/1944 Freetown 22/08/1944 Cape Town 8 5 Cape Town South Africa
27/08/1944 Cape Town 03/09/1944 Freetown 7 1 Freetown Sierra Leone
04/09/1944 Freetown 13/09/1944 Gourock 9 5 Gourock Scotland
18/09/1944 Gourock 25/09/1944 New York 7 10 New York USA
05/10/1944 New York 13/10/1944 Gourock 8 5 Gourock Scotland USA Troops to Europe
18/10/1944 Gourock 25/10/1944 Boston 7 16 Boston USA
10/11/1944 Boston 17/11/1944 Gourock 7 4 Gourock Scotland USA Troops to Europe
22/11/1944 Gourock 30/11/1944 New York 8 4 New York USA
04/12/1944 New York 12/12/1944 Gourock 8 6 Gourock Scotland USA Troops to Europe
18/12/1944 Gourock 25/12/1944 Halifax 7 9 Halifax Canada
03/01/1945 Halifax 09/01/1945 Gourock 6 5 Gourock Scotland USA Troops to Europe
14/01/1945 Gourock 22/01/1945 New York 8 6 New York USA
28/01/1945 New York 29/01/1945 Halifax 1 3 Halifax Canada
01/02/1945 Halifax 07/02/1945 Gourock 6 7 Gourock Scotland USA Troops to Europe
14/02/1945 Gourock 21/02/1045 Halifax 7 5 Halifax Canada
26/02/1945 Halifax 04/03/1945 Liverpool 7 4 Liverpool UK USA Troops to Europe
08/03/1945 Liverpool 16/03/1945 New York 8 22 New York USA
07/04/1945 New York 16/04/1945 Gourock 9 6 Gourock Scotland USA Troops to Europe
22/04/1945 Gourock 01/05/1945 Port Said 11 2 Port Said Egypt
03/05/1945 Port Said 16/05/1945 Fremantle 13 2 Fremantle Australia
18/05/1945 Fremantle 23/05/1945 Sydney 5 12 Sydney Australia
02/06/1945 Sydney 15/06/1945 Durban 13 4 Durban South Africa
19/06/1945 Durban 21/06/1945 Cape Town, South Africa
22/06/1945 Cape Town 29/06/1945 Freetown Sierra Leone
30/06/1945 Freetown 07/07/1945 Liverpool UK
18/07/1945 Liverpool 24/07/1945 Halifax, Canada
25/07/1945 Halifax 27/07/1945 New York USA21/08/1945 New York 01/09/1945 Southampton UK
02/09/1945 Southampton 03/09/1945 Rotterdam

The Hero Returns to Rotterdam

The *Nieuw Amsterdam* set sail from Southampton on 9 April 1946. Her destination was her home port of Rotterdam. The battered city of Rotterdam symbolised, perhaps more than anything, the part the Dutch people had played in freeing the Netherlands during the Second World War. Now nine years to the day of the anniversary of the launch of the *Nieuw Amsterdam*, she returned to Rotterdam like a conquering hero.

For some days prior the people of Rotterdam and the Netherlands had suppressed their excitement about welcoming home their national flagship. When the day of her arrival came, literally everything that could float in Rotterdam clustered around the great national liner. Her first appearance on the skyline with a dramatic backdrop of threatening black storm clouds was met with cheers as the sun shone down on her grey war weary decks. The river banks, from sea to port, heaved with cheering crowds with children proudly waving the Dutch Tricolour flag, shouting, 'The Darling of the Dutch!'. No ship in the history of the Dutch nation has ever received such a warm welcome and ovation.

Looking rust-stained, the *Nieuw Amsterdam* saluted the people of Rotterdam and the Netherlands with several deafening blasts from her whistles, which echoed amongst the bombed ruins of the city. As the tugs manoeuvred her alongside the pier, the maritime pride of the nation stood almost motionless for a dramatic moment before making actual contact with the shore. At this point the waiting crowd roared with delight and the waiting band proudly struck up with the 'Wilhelmus', the national anthem of the Netherlands. Along the waterfront people cheered and cried in great pride and celebration that their national hero had returned safely home.

Restoration and Rebirth

Shortly after the triumphant return of the *Nieuw Amsterdam* to Rotterdam in April 1946, she was transferred to her builders, the Rotterdam Dry Dock Company. The first task was to undertake a complete assessment and inspection of the ship from top to bottom, which resulted in a thirty-eight-page list. The first stage of the conversion and restoration of the ship commenced lasting fifteen weeks. This involved the removal of all troop equipment and fittings, such as: kitchens, wash places, alarm installations, bunks and standees. The thirty-six guns had been decommissioned and removed from the ship in Southampton, prior to the return of the ship. During the removal of bedding from a former troop dormitory a large stash of hidden US Dollars was discovered under a mattress, no doubt the winnings from a poker game left in error by a US GI. With true Dutch generosity the workers donated their discovery of cash to the Dutch Orphans Fund.

By the beginning of August 1946, the vessel was ready for stage two, the rebuilding. In the preceding February, March and April, 2,000 tons of furniture and internal decoration removed from the ship at the outbreak of war was returned to Rotterdam. Upon inspection many of the returned items were considered to be in poor condition. There were over 3,000 chairs and 500 tables for instance. These were sent back to the original manufacturers for repair, reconditioning and reupholstering. Of these, approximately 20 per cent had deteriorated so much that replacement was the only option. Factories and workshops all over the Netherlands scoured their storage facilities for material and fabrics, much of which had been secretly concealed from the Germans during the occupation. In several instances, small metal parts, such as door hinges and clamps, had to be redesigned and made by hand because machinery for their manufacture had been stolen by the enemy and transported to the industrial German Ruhr factories for war production.

The entire rubber flooring of the *Nieuw Amsterdam* was removed, as was 85 per cent of the carpeting. All steel work was scaled and preserved with all pipes throughout the ship cleaned or replaced. Elsewhere on the vessel all ceilings and walls were removed as many of the walls had the initials and messages of soldiers carved in. Perhaps the most common of which was 'Kilroy was here', along with an indiscreet drawing of a US GI. Despite discouraging shortages of material and skilled labour, all closets and fixtures in cabins and all of the ship's 374 private bathrooms were entirely replaced with new equipment. In the 268 first-class cabins the irremovable wooden panelling, which had been scarred, scratched and mutilated was planed down by carpenters to half of its original thickness, then repolished and varnished. Alongside all this activity by the chippies, the electricians set to work renewing all wiring and fuse boxes throughout the ship, which was a stupendous task involving over 300 miles of new electrical cable.

Perhaps one of the most challenging assignments during the restoration of the *Nieuw Amsterdam* was given to the glaziers, who had to replace or restore 12,000sq.ft of glass. Much of the original glass it was discovered had been painted over for blackout purposes in 1940 or had cracked in

Above: A proud occasion at New York with the first post-war arrival of the SS *Nieuw Amsterdam* on 6 November 1947. The Ambassador to the Netherlands Dr. Eelco Van Kleffens welcomes the Master of the *Nieuw Amsterdam* Commodore Anthony Dekema, whilst the smiling representative of the Mayor, Fredrick G Reinicke, looks on. (Associated Press)

Above centre: Gisny Buursink, a 25-year-old telephonist and secretary aboard the SS *Nieuw Amsterdam*, is pictured cooling off on the decks of the ship at New York on 16 May 1951. The sailors repainting the funnel appear to have forgotten the work in hand. (Associated Press)

Above right: Captain Cornelis M Snellman, Master of the SS Nieuw Amsterdam, smiles for the camera on 4 October 1962, soon after arrival in New York. He was a well liked and very popular man with all who sailed with him. (Associated Press)

the tropical sun. Hindrances to the glaziers were the workers who were busy removing and replacing the decks with 2,700sq.ft of teakwood. Alongside this army of deck workers were their colleagues who scraped free all the rails of carved initials. Down below a team of craftsmen set about removing all the perished rubber packing for the 2,200 portholes and replacing them like for like with new packing. The entirety of the brass work was reburnished.

New innovative improvements were made to the *Nieuw Amsterdam* to prepare her for the expected post-war boom. Air conditioning was installed to serve the two motion picture theatres, barber shops, beauty parlours and three dining rooms. The new revolutionary system was operated entirely by electricity and was capable of producing cooled air equivalent to an amount given off daily by 300 tons of melted ice. This innovation was expected to be very popular when cruising in the Caribbean. New safety improvements were introduced to the ship including 3,600 sprinklers providing instantaneous extinguishing and simultaneous automatic ringing alarms bells. In addition, 125 new hand extinguishers were installed at regular distances throughout the ship. In the boiler room there was a special carbon dioxide extinguishing system installed besides the steam and foam apparatus. Even the cargo holds were fitted with new Lux Rich smoke and fire protection detectors, which were connected to the bridge. All this new safety equipment was not lost on the designers of the future SS *United States* and many of the ideas and innovations were copied for this high-speed American super-liner of the Atlantic.

The boilers were completely reconditioned with total replacement of tubes, new stays, foundation rings and brick arches. After hydraulic and steam testing a twice-working psi they were found to be as good as new. The propeller blades were replaced and all mechanical gearing and propulsion engine room equipment overhauled. After the fitting and lubrication of the gigantic, smooth propeller blades, a single Dutch shipyard worker was filmed testing them; they could be turned freely.

One striking change was that the first-class grand hall now had a cocktail bar balcony at one end and a musicians' gallery at the other. Additionally several new luxury features were incorporated in the *Nieuw Amsterdam* upon her return to service with the installation of a second cinema, a third swimming pool and a tropical bar. These innovations were clearly intended at a future lucrative post-war cruise market.

At the conclusion of restoration and the post-war refit, the *Nieuw Amsterdam* sailed to the King George V Graving Dock at Southampton for final fitting out. Fourteen months after her return to Rotterdam, at a total cost of 12 million Guilders (just 1 million Guilders less than she cost to build), the *Nieuw Amsterdam* was given her final eight coats of external paints supplied by Peacocks of Southampton and expertly applied by Fern Bussell and his team of painters, from red oxide to top-coat gloss. As she gently emerged from the graving dock, hauled by Red Funnel and Alexandra Towing Company tugs, the gleaming *Nieuw Amsterdam* looked magnificent and was now ready for her much anticipated return to service. Polished to perfection she majestically and gracefully paraded down Southampton Water and across the Solent to return home to Rotterdam.

On 29 October 1947 Commodore Anthony Dekema, the master of the *Nieuw Amsterdam* gave the order to release all lines and the flagship of the Holland America Line set sail on her first post-war voyage to New York. Her special call sign was PGGF. With 1,256 passengers aboard, sixty-nine above of her normal capacity, she arrived to a hero's welcome in New York on 7 November. The great Dutch liner was greeted by the traditional fanfare of plumes of water cascading from Moran tug fireboats, plus hoards of cheering sightseers along the shores of Manhattan. Upon its arrival in New York the liner was greeted by the US ambassador to the Netherlands, Dr Eelco Van Kleffens, and the mayor of New York, William O'Dwyer.

Over the next few years the *Nieuw Amsterdam* developed a fine reputation on the North Atlantic and quickly won back her distinction and fame as one of the most popular liners. She quickly became a firm favourite of the rich and famous. On 28 June 1949, Dr Albert Schweitzer, the distinguished philosopher, physician, missionary, author and musician, arrived at Hoboken on board the *Nieuw Amsterdam*. He was making his way to appear at the GO Bicentennial Convocation at Aspen, Colorado. Dr Schweiter declared that 'sailing upon the *Nieuw Amsterdam* was one of the most pleasurable experiences of his life'. His sentiments were echoed by Hollywood screen sirens Rita Hayworth, Jane Russell and Katherine Hepburn. Katherine Hepburn said she found peace whilst sailing on the ship and enjoyed walks along the promenade deck in the fresh sea air. Other film stars like Spencer Tracey and Cary Grant vowed that travelling to Europe on the *Nieuw Amsterdam* was always their preferred option. Cary Grant was known to venture away from his exclusive suite whilst on board to drink and entertain the crew with impromptu one-man stand-up comedy routines. The ship was not the exclusive preserve of film stars, as royalty in the form of the king of Belgium, the Dutch royal family and HRH the Duke of Gloucester preferred the comfort of the *Nieuw Amsterdam*. The late Commodore Kleijn, who was master of the *Nieuw Amsterdam* in 1952, recalled that King Leopold of Belgium, who sailed with him on the *Nieuw Amsterdam* from Lisbon to Aruba, was fascinated with every aspect and detail of the ship. The king toured the ship from bridge to engine room meeting the crew and asking searching questions throughout the tour.

The Holland America Line reintroduced winter season cruising for the *Nieuw Amsterdam* in December 1947. This started with a cruise from New York to the West Indies. The programme of cruises proved to be very profitable with many wealthy Americans choosing to enjoy the comfort and pleasures aboard whilst experiencing the delights of the Caribbean sunshine. Although away for many weeks at a time, the Dutch crew benefited from generous tipping and many lived off their tips and banked their regular wages.

By 1952 the Nieuw Amsterdam's pre-war Holland America Line sister ships, the *Volendam* and the *Veendam*, were completely worn out. The Dutch shipping line therefore decided to invest in new replacements, the so called 'economy twins', *Ryndam* and *Maasdam*. The original designs of these two vessels were intended to be a combination of cargo-passenger freighters to complement the *Nieuw Amsterdam*, but the designs were changed when the construction commenced. The transatlantic service was further strengthened with the commissioning of the 24,294-ton intermediate tourist liner *Statendam (IV)* in February 1957. In 1956 the keel of *Rotterdam (V)* was laid, ready for launching in 1958 and completion in September 1959. By the late 1950s, Holland America's fleet was impressive by any standards, with the *Nieuw Amsterdam* at its heart.

When Commodore Kleijn retired in late 1952, he was succeeded by Commodore Pieter H.G. Verhoog, who in turn retired just twelve months later. Commodore Verhoog was known to be a great collector of Christopher Columbus material and many sketches, first editions and original works relating to the great explorer sailed with him, east bound across the Atlantic on the *Nieuw Amsterdam*.

Far left: The SS *Nieuw Amsterdam* pictured berthed at the Wilhelminakade, Rotterdam. Note the impressive Dutch barges in the foreground. (Gordon Turner/ Britton Collection)

Left: Dr Albert Schweitzer, the philosopher, physician, musician, missionary and author pictured arriving at New York on 28 June 1949 aboard the SS *Nieuw Amsterdam*. (Associated Press)

In 1956 the *Nieuw Amsterdam* was earmarked for modernisation and improvement. The air conditioning system was extended throughout all accommodation in the ship. New Denny Brown stabilisers were fitted to prevent rolling at sea and improve comfort, at the expense of fresh water tanks. The first class and tourist class rooms were fitted out for private facilities. The passenger numbers became 574 first class, 413 cabin class and 207 tourist class. Externally the new 'corporate image' was adopted as with the rest of the Holland America fleet, a new grey livery hull replacing the black. This was considered by many to be advantageous, as the lighter livery was more heat resistant when cruising in tropical climates. To many devoted followers of the *Nieuw Amsterdam* in New York and Europe, the change of livery was detrimental to her appearance. Her first voyage in the new grey livery was in January 1957 and thereafter she was scheduled for five New York to West Indies Caribbean cruises.

On 12 December 1958 the *Nieuw Amsterdam* was a day out of Southampton and after calling at Cobh in southern Ireland, she headed out west into the Atlantic increasing her speed to full ahead. An urgent radio message from the ship stated that there had been an accident aboard involving the master of the *Nieuw Amsterdam*, 60-year-old Captain Coenraad Bouman. He was seriously injured and had glass splinters in his left eye. The ship's surgeon thought it was too serious to deal with on board and so a decision was made to turn the *Nieuw Amsterdam* around and race back to Cobh to transfer the captain ashore. Happily Captain Bouman made a speedy recovery and was promoted to become commodore of the Holland America fleet. He planned to retire on 23 May 1961 after completing his final voyage on the *Nieuw Amsterdam*, but was persuaded to stay on until 29 September to be the first master of the new SS *Rotterdam*. During the maiden voyage of the *Rotterdam*, Coenraad Bouman was made an officer in the Order of Oranje Nassau, which he modestly considered to be an honour for the ship rather than himself.

During the severe winter of 1961–62, the *Nieuw Amsterdam* underwent a further major refit. The ship came out of service on Friday 13 October 1961 following an eastbound crossing from New York, for three months and the completion of the refit was undertaken in almost Arctic sub-zero temperatures with a snow covering. During the extensive refit, she was restyled as a first- and tourist-class ship, to operate in a similar fashion to the other two-class Holland America Line ships. The original cabin class was eliminated. This allowed her berthing arrangements to be more flexible to fit in with demand. From now on the accommodation outline could be either: 691 first class and 583 tourist class or 301 first class and 972 tourist class. Complete redecoration took place and the tourist class was greatly improved, with new public rooms, shops, a cinema and better private facilities. The board of Holland America Line made a radical economic decision to operate the *Nieuw Amsterdam* as a single-class ship while cruising to make her more competitive. In practice this meant that 750 passengers were accommodated for West Indies cruises and

Far left: Hollywood actress Rita Hayworth and her children Yasmin and Rebecca are pictured arriving on the SS *Nieuw Amsterdam* on 10 April 1955. (Associated Press)

Left: Actor Cary Grant was very fond of sailing aboard the SS *Nieuw Amsterdam* and is seen here with actress Betsy Drake. She was to become the actor's third wife. (Associated Press)

675 passengers for the Mediterranean cruises. The gross tonnage rose to 36,982.

The re-entry into service following the major refit was met with operational problems. The severe weather conditions of late December/ early January 1962 meant that the *Nieuw Amsterdam* encountered frozen seas with ice flows at Rotterdam, Le Havre and when heading up the Solent into Southampton. Blizzard-like conditions were experienced with a heavy snowfall covering the decks.

The year 1963 was to see some major changes with restructuring of the Holland America Line. It was decided to transfer operations from the traditional home at Hoboken across the river to Manhattan. The reason for this was that Manhattan was considered more accessible. Therefore Holland America redesigned Pier 40 at Houston Street and converted it to what was then by far and away the most modern passenger ship terminal on the New York waterfront. The new Pier 40, which was opened on Thursday 14 March 1963, had three berths. As a bonus there was an inner core parking facility and drive alongside drop-off points for passengers. Sadly this superb facility at Pier 40 was closed just over a decade later in November 1974 and reduced to a parking area. From March 1963 until September 1971 it was the regular docking point for the *Nieuw Amsterdam* when calling at New York.

On 4 January 1965, the *Nieuw Amsterdam* had a 'lucky escape' when she inadvertently rammed an unlit and unmanned railroad car float that was adrift a mile north of the Verrazano Narrows Bridge at the approach to New York. She had been returning with 827 passengers at the end of a cruise when the sudden collision occurred in the pre-dawn darkness. The impact of the collision caused five loaded freight wagons to somersault into the sea, whilst the ship suffered a 2ft gash in the starboard bow just ten feet above the waterline. The collision was felt throughout the ship as she was said to shudder. The *Nieuw Amsterdam* immediately stopped and after radioing through an account of what had happened she proceeded at dead slow ahead to Pier 40 in Manhattan. At daylight, divers were sent down to inspect any damage below the waterline. The slight hole above the waterline was quickly repaired and repainted allowing the *Nieuw Amsterdam* to sail as planned on her next voyage on 6 January.

On another occasion, whilst the *Nieuw Amsterdam* was resting at Pier 40 she was rocked by a fully loaded railroad car float, which was heading down the Hudson River. The impact at the stern of the ship caused the car float to almost bounce off, and several of the stern plates were dented as a result.

Red Funnel tug Captain John Davidson from Southampton recalls the *Nieuw Amsterdam* was like a smaller version of the Cunard RMS *Queen Elizabeth*. She was docked and undocked by at least three Southampton-based tugs from the Alexandra Towing Company and Red Funnel in a similar fashion to the Cunard RMS *Mauretania*. On occasions a sudden gust of wind could catch the docking procedure out. If the docking pilot, Captain Jack Holt, was aware of high winds and severe weather conditions he would request two additional support tugs, which usually included the Red Funnel tug *Calshot*. On more than one occasion, however, an easterly wind blowing up Southampton Water or across from the New Forest has hampered the docking of the *Nieuw Amsterdam*. Whilst entering the Ocean Dock with just one aft tug, a sudden gust of wind dangerously took the ship and she hit the quayside rubber buffers, as the tugs provided were found not to have enough power. The noise from

A beautiful aerial picture of the SS *Nieuw Amsterdam* pictured sailing past the Statue of Liberty at New York. (Britton Collection)

the side of the Dutch liner was like the sound of a squealing pig. Realising the gravity of the situation with a liner of this size out of control, the shore crew on the quayside and deck crew on board quickly responded. They exchanged securing lines to safely fasten the *Nieuw Amsterdam*. On the Bridge, the Trinity House Docking Pilot, Captain Jack Holt, turned to ashen faced Captain Cornelis Snellman and smiled, and quietly whispered, 'Well, that is one way to dock a liner!'

In April 1967 the *Nieuw Amsterdam* experienced trouble with one of her six boilers, which resulted in two cruises from New York being cancelled. The twin screw ship was propelled by two sets of four steam turbines connected to the shafts through single reduction gearing. However, the loss of a boiler severely handicapped the steam input required. The boiler was patched up, albeit the ship could continue at a reduced speed. However, the extra strain from the demand for steam by the remaining boilers had repercussions with tubes blowing and cracked stays. For the board of Holland America Line the temporary caulking of boiler tubes was no long-term solution. A more permanent outcome had to be found for if the *Nieuw Amsterdam* was to continue in service. The fate of the 29-year-old ship hung in the balance. The scheduled transatlantic voyages of 8 and 20 August 1967 were now cancelled, together with a twenty-two-day tropical Africa cruise. Further assessment of the boilers by the insurance inspector condemning two boilers, resulted in further Atlantic crossings on 18 September 1967 being cancelled. At this point, consideration was given at board level to offer the *Nieuw Amsterdam* for scrap and possibly acquire the Home Line's 27,644-ton *Oceanic* as a replacement. The *Oceanic* had been completed in March 1965 and was relatively new and could have made a worthy replacement, especially from a cruising point of view. On learning of this, some board members and Holland America crews reacted with requests to give the *Nieuw Amsterdam* more time whilst a satisfactory solution was found.

An urgent search of the world shipping market presented the answer. Five second-hand boilers were presented for sale. Two of the boilers originated from a war-built American cruiser that had seen only minimal service and had been mothballed. The cruiser was being cut up for scrap in California, and the two boilers were reserved and set aside for *Nieuw Amsterdam*. Three further boilers of the same design were discovered in US Navy storage and held in reserve. A decision was made there and then to purchase all five boilers and despatch them to the Wilton Fijenoord Shipyard at Schiedam. An immediate order was made to have them dispatched for transfer to Holland America's freighter *Moerdyk*, which upon receipt of the boilers sailed post haste.

Meanwhile the *Nieuw Amsterdam* was towed dead on 16 August by tugs and placed in Wilton's dry dock. Once they were in place, the engineers set about cutting a hole 23ft high by 33ft long in the shell plating on each side of the ship, using oxyacetylene torches. This allowed direct access to the boiler room from where five of the six original boilers were removed. On 21 August the first of the replacement boilers was installed on the portside, being carefully positioned alongside the one remaining original boiler that had been retained only as ballast. A second portside boiler followed in the same way as the first, after which the hole in the portside hull was sealed. The process was repeated on the starboard side of the ship, and within two days the three replacement starboard boilers were safely in position. The replacement boilers were connected up, hydraulically and steam tested to the satisfaction of the Insurance Inspector. The whole operation was the equivalent of a heart transplant.

Technical trials in the North Sea of the new steam plant followed between 30 November and 2 December. The result was a complete success and it was reported that the rejuvenated *Nieuw Amsterdam* steamed better than before. The new American boilers were however lighter than the originals and one less in number. The consequence of this was the necessity for the provision of extra ballast to compensate and maintain adequate stability. The new boilers gave the ship a cruising speed of 19.5 knots, which, although slower, was more economical. The twin shafts were rated at 15,000 shaft horsepower and they turned at 115rpm at full speed. The *Nieuw Amsterdam* now consumed 9.5 tons of Bunker C fuel an hour and her fuel capacity was 2,660 metric tonnes.

For the trial voyage over 250 invited guests were invited and representatives of the Holland America Line, including four senior directors. On the following westbound voyage across the Atlantic, which arrived in New York on 21 December, all went well.

The anchor of the SS *Nieuw Amsterdam* is given a spring cleaning at New York on 31 May 1969. (Associated Press)

The introduction of the Boeing 707 and De Havilland jet airliners flying over the Atlantic from 1958 introduced an element of competition that signalled the end of the age of the transatlantic ocean liner. In 1965 Cunard withdrew the RMS *Mauretania*, which was a former sister troopship in the Second World War. This was followed by the sale of the RMS *Queen Mary* in 1967 and RMS *Queen Elizabeth* in 1968. The *Nieuw Amsterdam* somehow managed to linger on with transatlantic crossings until September 1971. On several of her final season of voyages the crew were said to number more than the passengers being carried. The future looked uncertain and rumours circulated as to what would become of the *Nieuw Amsterdam*.

The Twilight Years of Cruising

In 1971 Holland America Line took the bold decision to devote the *Nieuw Amsterdam* to permanent cruising sailing, save that of positioning voyages, alongside the *Rotterdam* and *Statendam*. A significant economic but unpopular decision was also made to change the registration of the ship to Willemstad, Curaçao. The company's green-and white-banded yellow funnels were replaced by orange ones with a blue and white flash. The ship's call sign was also changed to PJRS and she now sailed under an Antillean flag.

A new career of full-time cruising was established for the *Nieuw Amsterdam* in her twilight years, sailing from Port Everglades in Florida to the Caribbean. The fourteen-day cruises took this proud classic liner to such exotic ports of call as Oranjestad and Aruba in the Netherlands Antilles, La Guaira and Pampatar in Venezuela, Fort-de-France in Martinique in the French West Indies and Charlotte Amalie in St Thomas in the US Virgin Islands. When cruising the Caribbean, the 800 cruise passengers had a choice of 314 outside cabins and 132 inside, the majority of which had private facilities. The ship benefited from already being fitted out with an almost universal air-conditioning system, which made passengers in tropical climates more comfortable.

At first the *Nieuw Amsterdam* was marketed as the largest cruise ship operating from Florida. On board, the Vanderbilt Dining Room was deleted from the list of public rooms and transferred to usage by the crew. Only the Champlain Dining Room, which could seat 640 passengers for dinner, was used. The kitchens of the *Nieuw Amsterdam* were the first on any liner in the world to be awarded the coveted *Chaîne des Rôtisseurs* of Paris. The renowned organisation of elite chefs supervised special courses and in-service training for the *Nieuw Amsterdam* staff before so honouring the ship. The cuisine was second to none and her reputation for a mountain of delicacies soon spread.

In the last few years of cruising the number of Dutch employees began to decrease, with more Asian crew members employed. On occasions the *Nieuw Amsterdam* would return home to Europe and undertake Arctic and Mediterranean cruises. All appeared to be going well for the *Nieuw Amsterdam* in her new cruising career and she was very popular. The fourteen-day Caribbean cruises were, however, reduced first to ten-day and later eight-day cruises.

The end, when it came, was brought about by a crisis in the Middle East. The Organisation of Petroleum Exporting Countries (OPEC), plus Egypt, Syria and Tunisia, raised the price of oil from $3 to $12 per barrel. The gas-guzzling, ever fuel-thirsty *Nieuw Amsterdam* just could not compete with this hard-hitting economic shock. Added to this were the large crew requirement and a rising outlay on wages. Very reluctantly, the board of the Holland America Line decided that she was now unprofitable and could not secure a good financial economic return. The board were presented with a disastrous set of financial figures for passenger operations with a $12.5 million loss as a result of escalating world fuel costs. It was therefore decided that the final revenue-earning voyage of the *Nieuw Amsterdam* would be from Port Everglades on 7 December 1973. A few old-faithful regular passengers managed to obtain reservations for the last cruise, which called at Willemstad (Curaçao), La Guaira (Venezuela), St George's (Grenada), Basse-Terre (Guadeloupe), Pointe-à-Pitre (Guadeloupe) and Charlotte Amalie (St Thomas). She returned to Port Everglades on 17 December and after disembarking her passengers the ship lay at anchor off Port Everglades with a skeleton crew to await a decision on her future.

A number of proposals were put to the board of Holland America Line to consider for the future of the *Nieuw Amsterdam*. These included conversion to a static high-class hotel, a floating casino and even a floating brothel! Tenders were also received for scrapping from three breakers. The decision was made to sell the once proud Dutch flagship to the Nan Feng Company of Kaohsiung, Taiwan for almost 13 million Guilders, which was a welcome addition to the bank account of the shipping line.

The news reached the ship of the decision of the board with shock and great sadness. Orders were received to prepare the ship to sail as quickly as possible for the delivery voyage. A steaming crew of sixty embarked, commanded by Captain R. ten Kate with Jaap Lievisse-Adriaanse as the chief engineer. The course of the final voyage entailed a brief call at Curaçao with a last westbound transit through the Panama Canal, before heading out into the Pacific for the final leg from Los Angeles to Kaohsiung. When the ship sailed from Port Everglades there was barely enough fuel in the bunkers to reach Curaçao. This was a bad time to purchase oil as the world fuel crisis was now at a peak and there were severe restrictions on availability at Curaçao. Numerous telephone calls resulted in the bland response, 'Sorry your requirement of fuel oil is unavailable.' The chief engineer decided to personally plead with the local oil company representatives to allow the ship to continue on the next leg of her funeral voyage.

The next fuel stop was at Los Angeles, but only a limited supply could be acquired here. The chief engineer decided to conserve fuel by sailing at just 12 knots using a minimum number of boilers. Elsewhere on the deserted ship other consumables were not in short supply. Many carcasses of meat, frozen fish and game, had not been transferred off the ship prior to sailing from Florida. One of the engineers decided to throw a feast for a king for all those on board to 'see the old girl out in style'. The challenge of how to go about cooking the large carcasses of meat without the use of the main gallery was solved by firing up one of the unused boilers and using it as a large oven. The feast was appreciated by all with large servings of rescued wines, champagne and spirits, including the chief engineer – that is until he discovered that his precious fuel oil reserve had been tapped to fire up a boiler!

Arrival in the pouring rain at Kaohsiung on 25 February 1974 was a depressing affair as the *Nieuw Amsterdam* joined a queue of some forty redundant ships awaiting their final fate. The condemned Dutch flagship waited for the final call which came on 2 March when breaking berth 57 became vacant. For the last time the *Nieuw Amsterdam* raised her anchor to move off to dock at demolition quay. As the ship approached the final end of her voyage it was clear that the local docking pilot was navigating at too high a speed and had lost complete control of the *Nieuw Amsterdam*. Captain Kate made a last-minute frantic attempt to intervene, but to no avail. There was a terrific grinding noise and a last shudder throughout the ship like the dying gasp of a slaughtered bull elephant on the plains of Africa. After expressing his dismay to the docking pilot that his ship had scraped along the side of the former Home Lines *Homeric*, Captain Kate fumed. The docking pilot replied: 'Any damage is of no consequence since the ship is doomed and in any case will never sail again.'

With the *Nieuw Amsterdam* at rest, the ship was signed over to Nan Feng and her Dutch crew flew home. Before leaving their beloved ship, the crew were allowed to remove a few souvenirs.

Over the next few weeks, local tradesmen invaded the *Nieuw Amsterdam* to pick over her like vultures. They secured the ship's artworks, furniture, fittings, cups, plates, cutlery and cooking equipment. Once all internal salvageable items and fittings were removed, the breaking of the hulk commenced on 16 May section by section. By early October, the last remains of the proud Dutch liner were no more.

Holland-America Line
NAME
STEAMER
SAILING
ROOM
PORT OF LANDING
CHECK WHERE BAGGAGE IS WANTED
IN STATEROOM
IN BAGGAGE ROOM
(Accessible at specified hours)
FIRST CLASS
CLAIM YOUR BAGGAGE FROM BAGGAGE MASTER BEFORE EMBARKATION
Printed in The Netherlands

Holland-America Line
NAME
STEAMER
SAILING
ROOM
PORT OF LANDING
CHECK WHERE BAGGAGE IS WANTED
IN STATEROOM
IN BAGGAGE ROOM
(Accessible at specified hours)
CRUISE
TO BE DELIVERED TO PIER 40, NORTH RIVER, FOOT OF WEST HOUSTON STREET, NEW YORK CITY
CLAIM YOUR BAGGAGE FROM BAGGAGE MASTER BEFORE EMBARKATION
Printed in The Netherlands

Holland-America Line
TOURIST CLASS
Holland-America Line
FIRST CLAS
Holland-America Line
CRUISE

HOLLAND-AMERICA LINE
PASSENGER
STEAMER
SAILING DATE
ROOM №
PORT OF LANDING
TOURIST CLASS
T
STATEROOM
PRINTED IN THE NETHERLANDS

Holland-America Line
Holland-America Line

Cor Alons: Leaded glass window, Tourist Class Children's Playroom. Architect Frits Spanjaard.

Cor Alons: Leaded glass window, Tourist Class Children's Playroom. Architect Frits Spanjaard.

Ruscha Wijdeveld: Leaded glass window Children's Play Deck, Cabin Class. Architect Frits Spanjaard.

Cor Alons: Leaded glass window, Third Class Bar. Architect Frits Spanjaard.

Holland-America Line
SOMETHING NEW IN FALL VACATIONS
14-DAY Luxury Cruise
TO SOUTH AMERICA and the WEST INDIES
S. S. NIEUW AMSTERDAM
From NEW YORK OCTOBER 16, 1952
Returning OCTOBER 30th
ST. THOMAS
LA GUAIRA
CURACAO
KINGSTON
HAVANA
Only
$335. UP
NO U.S. TRANS. TAX.

Holland America Line
A warm, friendly retreat — the First Class Smoking Room
Holland-America Line
"It's good to be on a well-run ship"
S.S. NIEUW AMSTERDAM
Agents:

SIXTH EDITION
MINIC SHIPS
Tri-ang
REG'D TRADE MARK
SHIPS
MINIC
1:1200 Scale diecast waterline models
NIEUW AMSTERDAM

Above: This is the original colour publicity photograph of the SS *Nieuw Amsterdam* sailing from New York with a backdrop of Manhattan. For many years this superb picture was exhibited on the wall of the Holland America Line office in New York until it was acquired by the author. The ship is named after the early Dutch settlement on Manhattan, founded as Fort Amsterdam in 1626, changed later to Nieuw Amsterdam. (Holland America Line/Britton Collection)

Right: A rare pre-war colour picture of the SS *Nieuw Amsterdam* dressed all over, complete with her black livery hull. (Richard Weiss Collection)

This is a very rare and possibly a unique colour photograph of the SS *Nieuw Amsterdam*, identified as being taken in the late afternoon of 5 September 1939 at Hoboken, New York. Note the 6ft-high letters 'Nieuw Amsterdam, Holland' on the side of the SS *Nieuw Amsterdam* prior to sailing. This was a precaution for sailing into the so-called 'war zone' to indicate Dutch neutrality. (Richard Weiss Collection)

This post-war colour picture of the SS *Nieuw Amsterdam*, taken in March 1953, shows her resting at her Holland America Line Hoboken berth at 5th Street Pier being refuelled with Bunker C oil. (David Boone/Britton Collection)

Sunrise at 5th Street Pier, Hoboken where the SS *Nieuw Amsterdam* is pictured in March 1953. (David Boone/Britton Collection)

The SS *Nieuw Amsterdam* is pictured underway, sailing from Le Havre in March 1953 escorted by local tug boats. (Britton Collection)

Left: A classic view from the decks of the SS *Nieuw Amsterdam* as she heads past Manhattan down the Hudson River in September 1953. (Britton Collection)

Bottom left: In this post-war view looking forward on the SS *Nieuw Amsterdam* we can see the new deck timbers and gleaming paintwork following the refurbishment of the ship in 1947. (Richard Weiss Collection)

Bottom right: The lonely figure of the forward look-out gazes back to the cameraman in this immediate post-war view of the SS *Nieuw Amsterdam*. Note the refurbished deck timbers and gleaming paintwork. Former crew members of the ship have dated this picture as possibly October 1947. (Richard Weiss Collection)

Above left: The post-war perfect way to relax when crossing the Atlantic was on the SS *Nieuw Amsterdam*. Passengers are pictured soaking up the sun on the Promenade Deck. (Richard Weiss Collection)

Left: New items of furniture were manufactured by Van Nie of Utrecht to replace damaged or lost interior furniture stored during the ship's troopship career during the Second World War. Here is a typical post-war Van Nie lounge set of table and chairs in observation lounge. Two thousand five hundred chairs and 550 tables were used in the public rooms aboard the ship, 1,050 chairs in passengers' cabins and 200 chairs in the crew's mess rooms. (Richard Weiss Collection)

Above: Passengers are pictured relaxing on the aft sun deck of the SS *Nieuw Amsterdam* during what is believed by the former crew to be a voyage in 1947. (Richard Weiss Collection)

Right: The fashions of the passengers pictured in this view of the aft sun deck of the SS *Nieuw Amsterdam* indicate that it could have been taken in the period between 1947 and the early 1950s. (Richard Weiss Collection)

Below: In this aft sun-deck view aboard the SS *Nieuw Amsterdam* taken in May 1950, we can clearly see the deck quoits markings painted on the timbers. (Gavin Whitelaw Collection)

Left: The exhausted crew of the SS *Nieuw Amsterdam* are pictured taking a well-earned rest during the Christmas Caribbean Cruise of 1947. According to the former crew members the ship was almost deserted as the passengers had gone ashore. The crew members pictured on the far left are thought to be fishing with a baited line. Did they have any success? After the Second World War the number of crew on board varied with the number of passengers, but was normally 695. (Richard Weiss Collection)

Below: Beauty beyond belief in the Bahamas as the SS *Nieuw Amsterdam* anchors off during the Christmas Caribbean Cruise of December 1950. This superb colour picture remained hidden and forgotten for almost 65 years at the former Holland America Line office in New York until discovered by the author. (Holland America Line/Britton Collection)

Right: In this breathtaking view taken during the Christmas Caribbean Cruise of December 1950, the SS *Nieuw Amsterdam* blends into the landscape. (Holland America Line/Britton Collection)

Below: This picture of the SS *Nieuw Amsterdam* taken in December 1950 was earmarked by the New York Publicity Officer of Holland America Line for use as a marketing and promotional tool. It lay buried and unseen in a filing cabinet in the New York office for almost 65 years and one wonders if the picture was ever used for its original purpose. (Holland America Line/Britton Collection)

Left: Another colour picture discovered in the former New York office of Holland America Line. This was the December 1950 publicity department view of the SS *Nieuw Amsterdam* berthed at Rotterdam. Discovered along with the colour slides and publicity materials was a box of original 16mm colour films of the SS *Nieuw Amsterdam* taken at the time. All were saved from oblivion and the hands of a New York trash man! (Holland America Line/Britton Collection)

Below: This stunning colour view of the SS *Nieuw Amsterdam* sailing from Rotterdam in December 1950 must have been used by the Holland America Line publicity and marketing department in the 1950s. The accompanying scribbled notes simply say: 'postcard, calendar and brochure'. (Holland America Line/Britton Collection)

Top left: A starboard aft deck view on the SS *Nieuw Amsterdam* taken in 1951. The golden glow of the sun perfectly reflects on the funnel as the ship enters New York. (Britton Collection)

Above: Mid-Atlantic deck quoits aboard the SS *Nieuw Amsterdam* in 1953. (Britton Collection)

Left: The Eastern Seaboard of the United States of America comes into view on the horizon from the upper forward observation deck of the SS *Nieuw Amsterdam* in 1953. (Britton Collection)

Below: The aft swimming pool aboard the SS *Nieuw Amsterdam*, mid-Atlantic in 1953. (Britton Collection)

Right: A view of the lifeboat promenade deck in October 1970 during a latter-day Scandinavian cruise. (World Ship Society)

Below right: Evening musical entertainment in the Grand Hall of the SS *Nieuw Amsterdam* in 1953. The two-deck high Grand Hall was 73 feet long and 52 feet wide. It had entrance doors of transparent glass and stainless steel, above which was a musician's gallery, enclosed with large glass ornamental leaves. Twenty engraved glass windows extended from floor to ceiling and were curtained by full-length crimson drapes to correspond with the banquettes which lined the sides. (Britton Collection)

Far left: Silly hat time aboard the SS *Nieuw Amsterdam* in 1953. (Britton Collection)

Left: The first-class mid-Atlantic Gala Buffet feast aboard the SS *Nieuw Amsterdam* in 1953. (Britton Collection)

Below left: First-class service remained a constant expectation aboard the SS *Nieuw Amsterdam* and this was evident during the Scandinavian cruise in October 1970. (World Ship Society)

Left and above: Fresh lobster and champagne is served aboard the SS *Nieuw Amsterdam* during the Christmas Caribbean Cruise of December 1950. (Holland America Line/Britton Collection)

Above: This Holland America Line Publicity Department colour picture of the exquisite ebony and bronze stairway in the first class was used to illustrate promotion material for the SS *Nieuw Amsterdam*. Sadly after almost 65 years in store the original is beginning to deteriorate. (Holland America Line/ Britton Collection)

Above right: A rare pre-war Holland America Line publicity department (New York Office) colour view of the Ritz-Carlton Café aboard the SS Nieuw Amsterdam taken on the February 1939 South America Cruise. Two thousand five hundred chairs and 550 tables were used in the public rooms aboard the ship, 1,050 chairs in passengers' cabins and 200 chairs in the crew's mess rooms. (Holland America Line/Britton Collection)

Right: A rare pre-war Holland America Line publicity department (New York Office) colour view of the Champlain Dining Room aboard the SS *Nieuw Amsterdam* taken on the February 1939 South America Cruise. (Holland America Line/Britton Collection)

Left: A rare pre-war Holland America Line publicity department (New York Office) colour view of the first class smoking lounge aboard the SS *Nieuw Amsterdam* taken on the February 1939 South America Cruise. (Holland America Line/ Britton Collection)

Right: A rare pre-war Holland America Line publicity department (New York Office) colour view of the first class cinema aboard the SS *Nieuw Amsterdam* taken on February 1939 South America Cruise. (Holland America Line/Britton Collection)

A rare pre-war Holland America Line publicity department (New York Office) colour view of the Grand Hall aboard the SS *Nieuw Amsterdam* taken on the February 1939 South America Cruise. The two-deck high Grand Hall was 73ft long and 52ft wide. It had entrance doors of transparent glass and stainless steel, above which was a musician's gallery, enclosed with large glass ornamental leaves. Twenty engraved glass windows extended from floor to ceiling and were curtained by full length crimson drapes to correspond with the banquettes which lined the sides. The carpeted area of the ship was 129,120 square feet with the most luxurious carpeting being fitted in the Grand Hall. (Holland America Line/ Britton Collection)

Both images left: Members of the SS *Nieuw Amsterdam* entertainment crew are pictured in action on the deck during a pole pillow fight. (Britton Collection)

Below left: Female first-class passengers on the SS *Nieuw Amsterdam* are pictured in action on the deck during a pole pillow fight in 1953. (Britton Collection)

Below: The first-class smoking room pictured in October 1970. Note the fine walnut panelling and plush leather seating. (World Ship Society)

Above: The lonely figure of the barman goes about his never-ending cleaning duties in the cocktail lounge in this October 1970 view. (World Ship Society)

Right: Midnight in the cocktail lounge aboard the SS *Nieuw Amsterdam* in October 1970. This cocktail bar was panelled in rosewood, with a black ceiling, in the centre of which was a compass, supported by a moulded brass fish. The brass door handles were fashioned as mermaids. (World Ship Society)

The deserted smoking lounge in October 1970. (World Ship Society)

The air conditioned cinema could accommodate 350 passengers and is pictured here in October 1970. (World Ship Society)

A Holland America Line publicity department view of the interiors taken in February 1939 during the South America Cruise. (Holland America Line New York Publicity Department/Britton Collection)

An extract from the SS *Nieuw Amsterdam* launch brochure showing the lead glass windows as fitted in 1938. (Holland America Line/Britton Collection)

Passengers relax in their deck chairs on the promenade deck mid-Atlantic in August 1957. The clock reads 11.35 a.m. All 60 clocks on the ship were controlled by a master clock on the bridge. The total surface area of portholes and deck windows on the SS *Nieuw Amsterdam* was 17,000 square feet. The thickness of the glass varied from $^{3}/_{8}$ in to 1in. All glass panels throughout the ship were replaced after the war. Amidships on the lower promenade deck and main deck there were 272 windows of Stone's stirrup type. These opened by turning a pivot. (Britton Collection)

The enclosed forward observation deck was always a favourite place for passengers to gather. In this view taken in October 1970, the ship is at sea heading north towards the Fjords of Norway. (World Ship Society)

Above: According to a distinguished British poet, 'The air up here was like wine.' In this view taken in October 1970, the ship is at sea heading north towards the Fjords of Norway. (World Ship Society)

Right: In this view, taken in October 1970, the photographer has somehow been allowed out to take a picture in what the crew referred to as, 'the Holy of Holies' on the forward deck, which was usually out of bounds for passengers. (World Ship Society)

Below: The Gymnasium in October 1970, complete with a rowing machine and exercise bikes. A solarium adjoined the gymnasium and an elevator connected directly with the swimming pool and Turkish baths on E Deck, nine decks below. (World Ship Society)

Right: The Children's Play Room aboard the SS *Nieuw Amsterdam*. (Britton Collection)

Above left: The bridge of the SS *Nieuw Amsterdam* in September 1963. (Britton Collection)

Above: SS *Nieuw Amsterdam* navigation officers peer out ahead to set a course. (Holland America Line)

Left: In this Holland America Line New York Publicity Department picture, the crew members are pictured on the Bridge of the SS *Nieuw Amsterdam* in a rather posed stance. This staged pictured was actually taken at Hoboken while the ship was at berth! The Bridge was a cosy place equipped with a magnetic steering compass, Gyro compass with 'Metal Mike' and course reader. (Holland America Line)

Above left: The Flying Bridge of the SS *Nieuw Amsterdam* in September 1963. Note the ship's lifeboat with the painted words 'Nieuw Amsterdam'. (Britton Collection)

Above: A rather unusual view taken on the Bridge of the SS *Nieuw Amsterdam* showing the navigation chart for a cruise voyage from New York. The course has been plotted in with a grid showing a record of progress with dates and map references. (Britton Collection)

Far left: A view of the Engine Room in the dark depths of the SS *Nieuw Amsterdam* in September 1963. The propelling machinery was twin-screw single reduction geared quadruple expansion turbines. These Schelde-Parsons turbines produced a shaft horsepower of 34,000. (Britton Collection)

Above: The builder's plate of the SS *Nieuw Amsterdam* taken in October 1970. (World Ship Society)

Above right: A member of the crew of the SS *Nieuw Amsterdam* is seen polishing the brass ship's bell with pride. (Britton Collection)

Right: The entrance to the new Holland America Line terminal building at Wilhelminakade, Rotterdam in October 1970, which was the starting point for the voyages of the SS *Nieuw Amsterdam*. (World Ship Society)

Above: A view looking forward from the observation deck of the SS *Nieuw Amsterdam* in October 1970 as the ship approaches the Wilhelminakade Terminal in Rotterdam. (World Ship Society)

Above right: A spectacular aerial view looking across the Port of Rotterdam showing the SS *Nieuw Amsterdam* at berth in the early 1960s. (Trevor Smyth/ Britton Collection)

Right: Fleetmates of the Holland America Line are pictured on parade at Wilhelminakade. (Britton Collection)

Right: A line of classic cars on the cobbled road and a canopy of trees mask the SS *Nieuw Amsterdam*, which is pictured at berth at the Wilhelminakade Terminal in Rotterdam. (Trevor Smyth/Britton Collection)

Below: A traditional Dutch barge passes the SS *Nieuw Amsterdam* which is pictured at berth at the Wilhelminakade Terminal in Rotterdam. (Trevor Smyth/ Britton Collection)

Below right: Viewed from the cobbled shore line opposite the Wilhelminakade Terminal in Rotterdam, we can see the SS *Nieuw Amsterdam* at berth in October 1970. (World Ship Society)

Left: A view from the observation lounge at the Wilhelminakade Terminal in Rotterdam in October 1970 showing the SS *Nieuw Amsterdam* preparing for passenger embarkation prior to a Scandinavian cruise. (World Ship Society)

Below: A small Dutch barge passes the SS *Nieuw Amsterdam* which is pictured at berth at the Wilhelminakade Terminal in Rotterdam in August 1967. (Marc Piche)

Waves, cheers and smiles from passengers on the deck of the SS *Nieuw Amsterdam* as she prepares to set sail in September 1963. (Britton Collection)

Away all lines, as the SS *Nieuw Amsterdam* sails from Rotterdam in October 1970. (World Ship Society)

Away all lines, as the SS *Nieuw Amsterdam* sails from Rotterdam in October 1970. (World Ship Society)

Viewed from the cobbled shore line opposite the Wilhelminakade Terminal in Rotterdam, we can see the SS *Nieuw Amsterdam* at berth in October 1970. (World Ship Society)

The first routine duty once underway on the SS *Nieuw Amsterdam* was the lifeboat drill, which is pictured here at Life Boat Station No.3 on the lifeboat deck. There were 22 sets of lifeboat davits of the Barclay Gravity type. The lifeboat gear was arranged so that the upper promenade deck was free from all obstacles and entirely available for passengers, chairs and deck games. (Britton Collection)

Above: Lifeboat drill on the SS *Nieuw Amsterdam*. There were 22 sets of lifeboat davits of the Barclay Gravity type. The lifeboat gear was so arranged that the upper promenade deck was free from all obstacles and entirely available for passengers, chairs and deck games. (Britton Collection)

Right: A spectacular bird's eye view looking down on the aft Open Promenade Sun & Sports Deck of the the SS *Nieuw Amsterdam.* (Holland America Line/ Britton Collection)

The SS *Nieuw Amsterdam* is pictured sailing down the New Waterway departing from Rotterdam in 1970. (World Ship Society)

Above left: The SS *Nieuw Amsterdam* is pictured sailing down the New Waterway departing from Rotterdam on 18 July 1970. (George Garwood/World Ship Society)

Above: Departure from Le Havre, taken from the SS *Nieuw Amsterdam* in September 1963. (Britton Collection)

Left: A rare unusual view taken from the Bridge of the SS *United States* at Le Havre showing the SS *Nieuw Amsterdam* just ahead preparing to sail. (Britton Collection)

This marvellous aerial view of the SS *Nieuw Amsterdam* sailing from Le Havre in September 1956 somehow found its way to the former New York office Publicity Department. It was earmarked for advertising and marketing but is believed to have been used as an illustration in an in-house calendar. (Holland America Line/ Britton Collection)

Above: The British Railways Southern Region Merchant Navy Class steam locomotive no. 35021 New Zealand Line is pictured waiting at Millbrook, Southampton with the Holland America Line Boat Train headboard. The Bulleid pacific steam locomotive is waiting to back down into the docks ready to haul the boat train express to London Waterloo on 10 May 1965. (J. R. Carter/Britton Collection)

Above right: The SS *Nieuw Amsterdam* is one of the very few liners to call at Southampton during the Seaman's Strike of May 1966. She is pictured here at berth in the New Docks. Being foreign crewed, the Dutch liner was exempt from industrial action. (Britton Collection)

Right: Viewed from Mayflower Park, the SS *Nieuw Amsterdam* is pictured arriving in Southampton in August 1965 escorted by Captain John Davidson's Red Funnel tug boat *Hamtun*. (Wilfred Robertson)

Above left: The inbound SS *Nieuw Amsterdam* is pictured off Dock Head, Southampton on 11 June 1970. (Nigel V Robinson)

Above: The Alexander Towing Co. tug *Romsey* takes the strain as the SS *Nieuw Amsterdam* sails from Southampton in the summer of 1960. (Marc Piche)

Left: Whilst berthed in Southampton the opportunity was taken to freshen up the paintwork on the SS *Nieuw Amsterdam* and the brave painters lowered aboard precariously alongside. The total number of portholes and sidelights was 1062. Amidships on the lower promenade deck and main deck there were 272 windows of Stone's stirrup type. These opened by turning a pivot. (Britton Collection)

Above left: A Blue Funnel Line sight seeing pleasure craft packed with tourists is pictured slowly passing the SS *Nieuw Amsterdam* at Southampton on 27 August 1970. (World Ship Society)

Above: The SS *Nieuw Amsterdam* is captured in all her glory being turned by the Red Funnel tug *Calshot* soon after departure sailing from Ocean Dock on 1 July 1969. (Jim McFaul/ World Ship Society)

Left: Alexander Towing Company and Red Funnel tug boats are pictured assisting the departing SS *Nieuw Amsterdam* in Ocean Dock, Southampton on 1 June 1968. (Nigel V. Robinson)

Left: According to Captain John Davidson on the Red Funnel tug *Hamtun*, a strong westerly wind was blowing when this picture was taken on 1 May 1967. This necessitated the provision of extra tug assistance for the SS *Nieuw Amsterdam* and Southampton Docking Pilot Captain Jack Holt sent instructions for the Dutch ship to be meet by six tugs. She is seen here flanked by two Red Funnel tugs and an Alexander Towing tug, but Captain Davidson recalled that this was duplicated with an additional three tugs on the other side of the ship, which are out of view. (World Ship Society)

Below: A brace of Red Funnel tugs, *Chale* and *Hamtun*, escort the SS *Nieuw Amsterdam* away from Southampton on 1 June 1968. (Nigel V. Robinson)

The SS *Nieuw Amsterdam* slowly glides down Southampton Water escorted by a Red Funnel tug. Note the open shell door in the SS *Nieuw Amsterdam*. (Barry J. Eagles)

The SS *Nieuw Amsterdam* cautiously enters Southampton Docks at Dead Slow Ahead speed assisted by a Red Funnel tug boat. (Barry J. Eagles)

With Hythe Pier in the background, the SS *Nieuw Amsterdam* is seen sailing from Southampton in the early evening of 21 August 1971 assisted by the Red Funnel tug boat *Calshot*. (Britton Collection)

The outbound SS *Nieuw Amsterdam* escorted by a single Red Funnel tug boat is seen sailing down Southampton Water past the Fawley Oil Refinery in July 1969. Passing inbound in the opposite direction is a Red Funnel ferry from Cowes. (World Ship Society)

This superb aerial view of the SS *Nieuw Amsterdam* shows her heading out into the Atlantic off the west coast of Ireland with nothing ahead but clear blue seas. (World Ship Society)

Above: The sea breeze on the life boat deck catches the lady's skirt heading out into the Atlantic from the west coast of Ireland. (Gavin Whitelaw)

Right: This is the spectacular view looking down the life boat deck of the SS *Nieuw Amsterdam* as she begins to increase speed away from Cobh in Ireland heading west out into the Atlantic. Next stop: New York. (Britton Collection)

Left: Full steam ahead westbound across the Atlantic on the SS *Nieuw Amsterdam* in the summer of 1965. A view from the Flying Bridge looking aft across the line of lifeboats with those two magnificent funnels gleaming in the August sunlight. The ship is purring and gliding across the calm seas. Each funnel carried one electrically operated steam whistle. In addition a special foghorn of the Jessen howler type was installed in the bow which could be heard for a distance of 15 miles, but was inaudible inside the ship. (Britton Collection)

Below left: Threatening dark storm clouds shroud the SS *Nieuw Amsterdam* above as she sweeps across the Atlantic in July 1963. (Britton Collection)

Below: Underway on the SS *Nieuw Amsterdam* in October 1970. The service speed of the ship was 21 ½ knots, which enabled her to cross the Atlantic from Southampton to New York in six days. (World Ship Society)

Above: The SS *Nieuw Amsterdam* has slowed and is greeted by a US Coast Guard vessel alongside, off the Eastern Seaboard of the United States of America prior to entering New York. The New York docking pilot awaits transfer along with customs officers. (Gavin Whitelaw)

Right: The SS *Nieuw Amsterdam* fights her way up an icy Hudson River at New York prior to docking at her Holland America Line Hoboken berth at 5th Street Pier. The temperature is well below zero as the inky exhaust from the ship's funnels lingers in the polluted air. (Britton Collection)

Left: This is a rare and now historic exterior view of the Holland America Line 5th Street Pier on 3 November 1959. This once familiar and nostalgic scene is completed by a New York cop and a distinctive yellow cab. (Richard Weiss Collection)

Below left: This is rare and now historic interior view of the Holland America Line 5th Street Pier on 3 November 1959. (Richard Weiss Collection)

Below: Demolition and destruction at the depressing vandalised remains of the once proud Holland America Line 5th Street Pier at Hoboken. (Britton Collection)

The SS *Nieuw Amsterdam* rests at berth at the Holland America line 5th Street Pier at Hoboken, her regular home for so many years. The pointed tip of the Empire State Building can just be seen protruding above the pier. The scene is completed by a fine display of classic cars. (Richard Weiss Collection)

A Brooklyn car ferry pauses in the Hudson River at New York to make way for the SS *Nieuw Amsterdam* as she sails past with a backdrop of Manhattan behind her. (Britton Collection)

A smoky departure from 5th Street Pier, Hoboken in September 1963. The SS *Nieuw Amsterdam* is assisted by a Moran tug boat. (Britton Collection)

The Holland America Line New York publicity and marketing department chartered a local helicopter to take a series of colour slide aerial views of the SS *Nieuw Amsterdam* sailing from New York in August 1962. This aerial view is a personal favourite and shows her accompanied by a Moran tug boat making her way down the Hudson River. It is believed to have been used in the mid-1960s as a Holland America Line calendar illustration circulated to travel agents. (Holland America Line/Britton Collection)

Looking every inch a classic liner, the SS *Nieuw Amsterdam* is seen slowly sailing down the Hudson River in New York in April 1958. (Marc Piche)

Above: A breath-taking view of the SS *Nieuw Amsterdam* is just about to pass under the impressive Verrazzano Bridge at the entrance to New York Harbour in April 1966. (Britton Collection)

Above right: The SS *Nieuw Amsterdam* heads through the Narrows near the construction site of the Verrazzano Bridge in August 1958. (Britton Collection)

Right: Quayside in the Caribbean in 1971. (Britton Collection)

Above: The curbside sign says, 'No fishing', but that does not deter the locals. The SS *Nieuw Amsterdam* is pictured at Port Everglades, Fort Lauderdale in the USA and a plume of steam rises from her forward funnel indicating that she is ready to sail. (Britton Collection)

Above right: A traditional Caribbean steel band welcome awaits the SS *Nieuw Amsterdam* which is pictured anchored off in this tropical paradise. (Britton Collection)

Right: The SS *Nieuw Amsterdam* is pictured during her cruising career when based in Florida, USA. Her unique charm remained to the end, although she rarely crossed the Atlantic in her twilight years. (Barry J. Eagles)

Above: A Caribbean parade of classic liners at the idyllic tropical setting of Port-au-Prince in 1958, from left to right: Cunard RMS *Mauretania*, Holland America Line SS *Nieuw Amsterdam* and the French Line *Liberté*. (Britton Collection)

Above right: Former wartime troopships: left the Holland America Line SS *Nieuw Amsterdam* and right the North German Lloyd TS *Bremen* (the former SS *Pasteur*) are anchored off Port-au-Prince in January 1961. A tender to convey passengers from ship to shore is seen approaching the *Nieuw Amsterdam* which has portable gangways slewed from the ship's side. (Britton Collection)

Right: The New York office of the Holland America Line publicity and marketing department arranged for a series of aerial pictures to be taken at Curacao from an Auster light aircraft in December 1960. These pictures were used to advertise and promote future Caribbean cruises of the SS *Nieuw Amsterdam*. (Holland America Line/Britton Collection)

Above: A view looking back from the ship-to-shore tender showing the SS *Nieuw Amsterdam* at anchor off Curaçao. (Britton Collection)

Above right: The ship to shore tender boat is gently lowered over the side as the SS *Nieuw Amsterdam* rests at anchor off Curaçao in March 1959. (Britton Collection)

Right: A tropical setting as the SS *Nieuw Amsterdam* rests at anchor in the Caribbean. (Britton Collection)

The SS *Nieuw Amsterdam* is securely tied to her moorings in Curaçao Harbour in March 1960. (A. Corriman/Britton Collection)

The life aid ring clearly shows that this picture of the SS *Nieuw Amsterdam* and the SS *Argentina* was taken from the deck of the SS *Empress of England* as she lay at anchor in the Caribbean in March 1960. (A. Corriman/Britton Collection)

The SS *Nieuw Amsterdam* is pictured in berth. On the quay alongside are fuel oil barrels and propane gas cylinders. Next to these explosives, a cook from the ship peers out through the shell door smoking a cigarette! (World Ship Society)

Below: The SS *Nieuw Amsterdam* is pictured safely at anchor at sea with a ship to shore tender alongside during a Caribbean cruise. In shore the tip of a dangerous reef protrudes through the waves. (Stan Tedford/Paul Boot Collection)

Above: A vast complex network of ropes secure the SS *Nieuw Amsterdam* in March 1970. Each of these 9 inch circumference manilla fibre ropes was 120 fathoms in length, weighed about 18 cwt and had a breaking strain of 31.5 tons. (A. Corriman/Britton Collection)

In this beautiful portrait of the SS *Nieuw Amsterdam* she is pictured berthed alongside the SS *Ariadne*. (World Ship Society)

Nothing ahead but clear blue seas. (World Ship Society)

Above and right: The two funnels on the SS *Nieuw Amsterdam* topped 147ft above the keel of the ship. Each funnel measured 41 feet from base to top with a diameter of 35ft and a circumference of 85 feet. The after funnel contained a complete set of fresh water filters with a capacity of 80 tons per hour, fuel tanks, sanitary tanks and suction ventilators for galley odours. Each funnel carried one electrically operated steam whistle. In addition a special foghorn of the Jessen howler type was installed in the bow which could be heard for a distance of 15 miles, but was inaudible inside the ship. (World Ship Society)

Above: A view of the deserted sports deck in October 1970. (World Ship Society)

Above right: Sunbathers appear to have taken over the aft sports deck in this view taken in October 1970. (World Ship Society)

Right: A panoramic view of the aft sun deck on the SS *Nieuw Amsterdam* in October 1970. (World Ship Society)

Right: The aft sun deck and swimming pool in 1970. (World Ship Society)

Below: Passengers relax in their deck chairs on the aft sun deck in 1953. (Britton Collection)

Below right: A few privileged passengers have been invited forward to take happy snaps as the SS *Nieuw Amsterdam* rests at anchor in the Caribbean in November 1970. (Britton Collection)

The crew take a well-deserved rest, sun bathing on the forward deck, as the SS *Nieuw Amsterdam* lay at anchor in the Caribbean in November 1970. After the Second World War the number of crew on board varied with the number of passengers, but was normally 695. (Britton Collection)

Don't sail without us! The sign at La Guaira informing passengers of the sailing time of the ship in November 1970. (Britton Collection)

The SS *Nieuw Amsterdam* masts had a height of 118ft from the deck and were placed at slightly divergent angles, for optical reasons. The tops of the masts were 175ft above the sea level. The crow's nest, which had a steel ladder inside the mast, was 95ft above sea level and had a telephone to the bridge. (World Ship Society)

A view of the stern of the SS *Nieuw Amsterdam* in October 1970 shows her dressed overall with the flag of the Netherlands proudly flying. Underneath the name *Nieuw Amsterdam* is her home port of registration, Rotterdam. (World Ship Society)

Above and below: The illuminated stern of the SS *Nieuw Amsterdam* at night was a magnificent sight to behold. (World Ship Society)

An on-deck charcoal grill buffet of beef burgers, sausages, sirloin steak and mushrooms aboard the SS *Nieuw Amsterdam* in October 1970. (World Ship Society)

The forward view from the SS *Nieuw Amsterdam* entering a Norwegian port with a tug leading her to the quayside in October 1970. (World Ship Society)

The portable gangway with the name Holland America Line is in place as passengers are welcomed back aboard for their cruise. (World Ship Society)

The stunning view from the stern as the SS *Nieuw Amsterdam* steams from a fjord in Norway during her Scandinavian cruise in October 1970. (World Ship Society)

Left: The stunning view looking over the bow as the SS *Nieuw Amsterdam* steams into a Norwigian fjord during her Scandinavian cruise in October 1970. (World Ship Society)

Below: The perfect Viking portrait photograph of the SS *Nieuw Amsterdam* at anchor in a Norwegian fjord cloaked in cloud but with a stunning reflection in the icy waters in October 1970. (Britton Collection)

Above: All alone! The SS *Nieuw Amsterdam* lay at berth in a Norwegian port in October 1970. (World Ship Society)

Right: The SS *Nieuw Amsterdam* cautiously enters port with officers and deck hands monitoring progress at the bow. (World Ship Society)

Above: On parade in October 1970: the SS *Nieuw Amsterdam*, P&O Line SS *Iberia* and British India Line SS *Uganda*. (World Ship Society)

Above right: A stern view as the SS *Nieuw Amsterdam* manoeuvres into the quayside shows the P&O Line SS *Iberia* and British India Line SS *Uganda* already at berth. (World Ship Society)

Right: Passengers gaze down from the decks of the SS *Nieuw Amsterdam* as a Norwegian girl's marching band waits quayside to salute her arrival. Waiting at berth next to the ship are the P&O Line *Iberia* and the British India Line educational cruise ship SS *Uganda*. (World Ship Society)

Nieuw Amsterdam demolition. (Kartsten Petersen)

Nieuw Amsterdam demolition. (Kartsten Petersen)

If you enjoyed this book, you may also be interested in…

ISBN 978 0 7509 6101 1

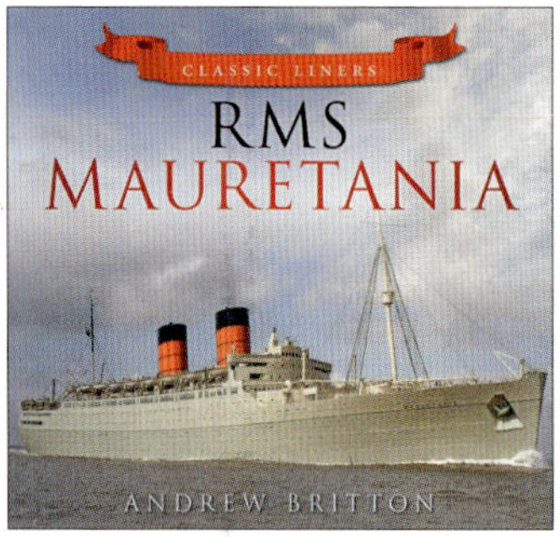

ISBN 978 0 7524 7950 7

ISBN 978 0 7524 9870 6

ISBN 978 0 7524 7952 1

ISBN 978 0 7524 9881 2

ISBN 978 0 7524 7953 8

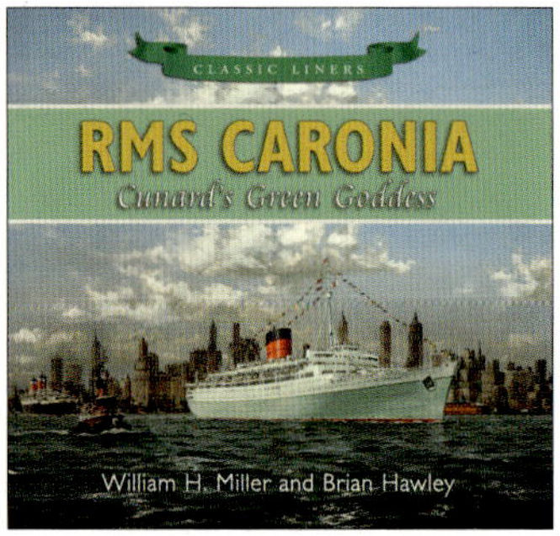

ISBN 978 0 7524 5791 8

ISBN 978 0 7524 7951 4

ISBN 978 0 7524 5662 1

Visit our website and discover thousands of other History Press books.

www.thehistorypress.co.uk

The History Press